Scott Foresman
Science

See learning in a whole new light

PEARSON
Scott
Foresman

Editorial Offices: Glenview, Illinois • Parsippany, New Jersey • New York, New York
Sales Offices: Boston, Massachusetts • Duluth, Georgia • Glenview, Illinois •
Coppell, Texas • Sacramento, California • Mesa, Arizona

Series Authors

Dr. Timothy Cooney
Professor of Earth Science and Science Education
University of Northern Iowa (UNI)
Cedar Falls, Iowa

Dr. Jim Cummins
Professor
Department of Curriculum, Teaching, and Learning
The University of Toronto
Toronto, Canada

Dr. James Flood
Distinguished Professor of Literacy and Language
School of Teacher Education
San Diego State University
San Diego, California

Barbara Kay Foots, M.Ed
Science Education Consultant
Houston, Texas

Dr. M. Jenice Goldston
Associate Professor of Science Education
Department of Elementary Education Programs
University of Alabama
Tuscaloosa, Alabama

Dr. Shirley Gholston Key
Associate Professor of Science Education
Instruction and Curriculum Leadership Department
College of Education
University of Memphis
Memphis, Tennessee

Dr. Diane Lapp
Distinguished Professor of Reading and Language Arts in Teacher Education
San Diego State University
San Diego, California

Sheryl A. Mercier
Classroom Teacher
Dunlap Elementary School
Dunlap, California

Dr. Karen L. Ostlund
UTeach
College of Natural Sciences
The University of Texas at Austin
Austin, Texas

Dr. Nancy Romance
Professor of Science Education & Principal Investigator
NSF/IERI Science IDEAS Project
Charles E. Schmidt College of Science
Florida Atlantic University
Boca Raton, Florida

Dr. William Tate
Chair and Professor of Education and Applied Statistics
Department of Education
Washington University
St. Louis, Missouri

Dr. Kathryn C. Thornton
Professor
School of Engineering and Applied Science
University of Virginia
Charlottesville, Virginia

Dr. Leon Ukens
Professor of Science Education
Department of Physics, Astronomy, and Geosciences
Towson University
Towson, Maryland

Steve Weinberg
Consultant
Connecticut Center for Advanced Technology
East Hartford, Connecticut

ISBN: 0-328-10006-4 (SVE); ISBN: 0-328-15676-0 (A); ISBN: 0-328-15682-5 (B); ISBN: 0-328-15688-4 (C); ISBN: 0-328-15694-9 (D)

5 6 7 8 9 10 V063 12 11 10 09 08 07 06

Consulting Author

Dr. Michael P. Klentschy
Superintendent
El Centro Elementary School District
El Centro, California

Science Content Consultants

Dr. Frederick W. Taylor
Senior Research Scientist
Institute for Geophysics
Jackson School of Geosciences
The University of Texas at Austin
Austin, Texas

Dr. Ruth E. Buskirk
Senior Lecturer
School of Biological Sciences
The University of Texas at Austin
Austin, Texas

Dr. Cliff Frohlich
Senior Research Scientist
Institute for Geophysics
Jackson School of Geosciences
The University of Texas at Austin
Austin, Texas

Brad Armosky
McDonald Observatory
The University of Texas at Austin
Austin, Texas

Content Consultants

Adena Williams Loston, Ph.D.
Chief Education Officer
Office of the Chief Education Officer

Clifford W. Houston, Ph.D.
Deputy Chief Education Officer for Education Programs
Office of the Chief Education Officer

Frank C. Owens
Senior Policy Advisor
Office of the Chief Education Officer

Deborah Brown Biggs
Manager, Education Flight Projects Office
Space Operations Mission Directorate, Education Lead

Erika G. Vick
NASA Liaison to Pearson Scott Foresman
Education Flight Projects Office

William E. Anderson
Partnership Manager for Education
Aeronautics Research Mission Directorate

Anita Krishnamurthi
Program Planning Specialist
Space Science Education and Outreach Program

Bonnie J. McClain
Chief of Education
Exploration Systems Mission Directorate

Diane Clayton, Ph.D.
Program Scientist
Earth Science Education

Deborah Rivera
Strategic Alliances Manager
Office of Public Affairs
NASA Headquarters

Douglas D. Peterson
Public Affairs Officer
Astronaut Office
Office of Public Affairs
NASA Johnson Space Center

Nicole Cloutier
Public Affairs Officer
Astronaut Office
Office of Public Affairs
NASA Johnson Space Center

Reviewers

Dr. Maria Aida Alanis
Administrator
Austin ISD
Austin, Texas

Melissa Barba
Teacher
Wesley Mathews Elementary
Miami, Florida

Dr. Marcelline Barron
Supervisor/K–12 Math
and Science
Fairfield Public Schools
Fairfield, Connecticut

Jane Bates
Teacher
Hickory Flat Elementary
Canton, Georgia

Denise Bizjack
Teacher
Dr. N. H. Jones Elementary
Ocala, Florida

Latanya D. Bragg
Teacher
Davis Magnet School
Jackson, Mississippi

Richard Burton
Teacher
George Buck Elementary
School 94
Indianapolis, Indiana

Dawn Cabrera
Teacher
E. W. F. Stirrup School
Miami, Florida

Barbara Calabro
Teacher
Compass Rose Foundation
Ft. Myers, Florida

Lucille Calvin
Teacher
Weddington Math &
Science School
Greenville, Mississippi

Patricia Carmichael
Teacher
Teasley Middle School
Canton, Georgia

Martha Cohn
Teacher
An Wang Middle School
Lowell, Massachusetts

Stu Danzinger
Supervisor
Community Consolidated
School District 59
Arlington Heights, Illinois

Esther Draper
Supervisor/Science Specialist
Belair Math Science
Magnet School
Pine Bluff, Arkansas

Sue Esser
Teacher
Loretto Elementary
Jacksonville, Florida

Dr. Richard Fairman
Teacher
Antioch University
Yellow Springs, Ohio

Joan Goldfarb
Teacher
Indialantic Elementary
Indialantic, Florida

Deborah Gomes
Teacher
A J Gomes Elementary
New Bedford, Massachusetts

Sandy Hobart
Teacher
Mims Elementary
Mims, Florida

Tom Hocker
Teacher/Science Coach
Boston Latin Academy
Dorchester, Massachusetts

Shelley Jaques
Science Supervisor
Moore Public Schools
Moore, Oklahoma

Marguerite W. Jones
Teacher
Spearman Elementary
Piedmont, South Carolina

Kelly Kenney
Teacher
Kansas City Missouri
School District
Kansas City, Missouri

Carol Kilbane
Teacher
Riverside Elementary School
Wichita, Kansas

Robert Kolenda
Teacher
Neshaminy School District
Langhorne, Pennsylvania

Karen Lynn Kruse
Teacher
St. Paul the Apostle
Yonkers, New York

Elizabeth Loures
Teacher
Point Fermin
Elementary School
San Pedro, California

Susan MacDougall
Teacher
Brick Community Primary
Learning Center
Brick, New Jersey

Jack Marine
Teacher
Raising Horizons Quest
Charter School
Philadelphia, Pennsylvania

Nicola Micozzi Jr.
Science Coordinator
Plymouth Public Schools
Plymouth, Massachusetts

Paula Monteiro
Teacher
A J Gomes Elementary
New Bedford, Massachusetts

Tracy Newallis
Teacher
Taper Avenue Elementary
San Pedro, California

Dr. Eugene Nicolo
Supervisor, Science K–12
Moorestown School District
Moorestown, New Jersey

Jeffrey Pastrak
School District of Philadelphia
Philadelphia, Pennsylvania

Helen Pedigo
Teacher
Mt. Carmel Elementary
Huntsville, Alabama

Becky Peltonen
Teacher
Patterson Elementary School
Panama City, Florida

Sherri Pensler
Teacher/ESOL
Claude Pepper Elementary
Miami, Florida

Virginia Rogliano
Teacher
Bridgeview Elementary
South Charleston,
West Virginia

Debbie Sanders
Teacher
Thunderbolt Elementary
Orange Park, Florida

Grethel Santamarina
Teacher
E. W. F. Stirrup School
Miami, Florida

Migdalia Schneider
Teacher/Bilingual
Lindell School
Long Beach, New York

Susan Shelly
Teacher
Bonita Springs Elementary
Bonita Springs, Florida

Peggy Terry
Teacher
Madison District 151
South Holland, Illinois

Jane M. Thompson
Teacher
Emma Ward Elementary
Lawrenceburg, Kentucky

Martha Todd
Teacher
W. H. Rhodes Elementary
Milton, Florida

Renee Williams
Teacher
Central Elementary
Bloomfield, New Mexico

Myra Wood
Teacher
Madison Street Academy
Ocala, Florida

Marion Zampa
Teacher
Shawnee Mission
School District
Overland Park, Kansas

Science

See learning in a whole new light

How are the living things around us alike and different?

What are the parts of a cell?

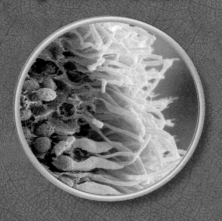

Chapter 3 • Reproduction

How do living things reproduce?

Chapter 4 • Body Systems

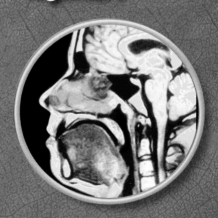

How do body parts work together?

Unit A Life Science

What processes take place in plants?

How do organisms live together in ecosystems?

Chapter 7 • Ecosystems

How do energy, organisms, and the environment interact?

Unit B Earth Science

How does the theory of plate tectonics explain Earth's landforms?

How do rocks and minerals form soils?

Chapter 8 • Plate Tectonics

Chapter 9 • Rocks and Minerals

Chapter 10 • Reshaping Earth's Surface

What processes change Earth's landforms?

How can we use Earth's resources wisely?

Chapter 11 • Earth's Resources

Chapter 12 • Climate and Weather

What causes Earth's weather and climate?

Unit C Physical Science

How can the properties of matter change?

What do the many types of matter have in common?

Chapter 13 • Matter

Chapter 14 • Building Blocks of Matter

Chapter 15 • Forces and Motion

How are motion and forces related?

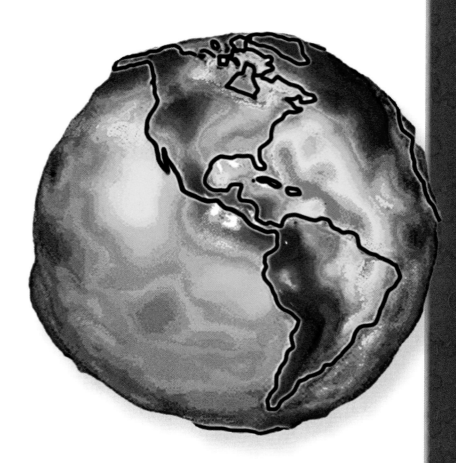

Unit C Physical Science

How do machines make work easier?

Chapter 16 • Machines

How can energy change from one form to another?

Chapter 17 • Changing Energy Forms

Chapter 18 • Thermal and Light Energy

How are thermal energy and light energy transferred?

Unit D Space and Technology

What are the effects of the movements of Earth and the Moon?

What is Earth's place in the universe?

Chapter 21 • Impacts of Technology

How can robots help us now and in the future?

How to Read Science

A page like this one is toward the beginning of each chapter. It shows you how to use a reading skill that will help you understand what you read.

Before Reading

Before you read the chapter, read the Build Background page and think about how to answer the question. Recall what you already know as you answer the question. Work with a partner to make a list of what you already know. Then read the How to Read Science page.

Target Reading Skill

Each page has one target reading skill. The reading skill corresponds with a process skill in the Directed Inquiry activity on the facing page. The reading skill will be useful as you read science.

Real-World Connection

Each page has an example of something you might read. It also connects with the Directed Inquiry activity.

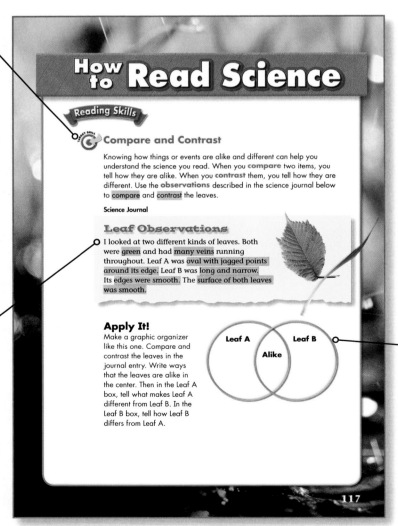

Graphic Organizer

A useful strategy for understanding anything you read is to create a graphic organizer. A graphic organizer can help you think about the information and relate parts of it to each other. Each reading skill has a certain graphic organizer.

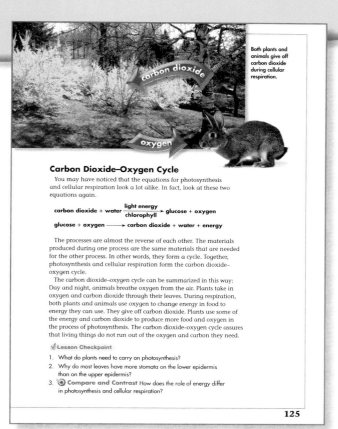

Both plants and animals give off carbon dioxide during cellular respiration.

Carbon Dioxide–Oxygen Cycle

You may have noticed that the equations for photosynthesis and cellular respiration look a lot alike. In fact, look at these two equations again.

$$\text{carbon dioxide} + \text{water} \xrightarrow[\text{chlorophyll}]{\text{light energy}} \text{glucose} + \text{oxygen}$$

$$\text{glucose} + \text{oxygen} \longrightarrow \text{carbon dioxide} + \text{water} + \text{energy}$$

The processes are almost the reverse of each other. The materials produced during one process are the same materials that are needed for the other process. In other words, they form a cycle. Together, photosynthesis and cellular respiration form the carbon dioxide–oxygen cycle.

The carbon dioxide–oxygen cycle can be summarized in this way: Day and night, animals breathe oxygen from the air. Plants take in oxygen and carbon dioxide through their leaves. During respiration, both plants and animals use oxygen to change energy in food to energy they can use. They give off carbon dioxide. Plants use some of the energy and carbon dioxide to produce more food and oxygen in the process of photosynthesis. The carbon dioxide–oxygen cycle assures that living things do not run out of the oxygen and carbon they need.

✓ Lesson Checkpoint

1. What do plants need to carry on photosynthesis?
2. Why do most leaves have more stomata on the lower epidermis than on the upper epidermis?
3. ◉ **Compare and Contrast** How does the role of energy differ in photosynthesis and cellular respiration?

125

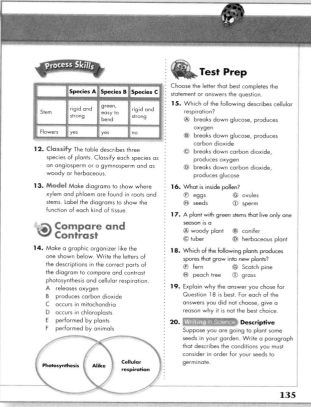

Process Skills

	Species A	Species B	Species C
Stem	rigid and strong	green, easy to bend	rigid and strong
Flowers	yes	yes	no

12. **Classify** The table describes three species of plants. Classify each species as an angiosperm or a gymnosperm and as woody or herbaceous.

13. **Model** Make diagrams to show where xylem and phloem are found in roots and stems. Label the diagrams to show the function of each kind of tissue.

◉ Compare and Contrast

14. Make a graphic organizer like the one shown below. Write the letters of the descriptions in the correct parts of the diagram to compare and contrast photosynthesis and cellular respiration.
   A releases oxygen
   B produces carbon dioxide
   C occurs in mitochondria
   D occurs in chloroplasts
   E performed by plants
   F performed by animals

Photosynthesis — Alike — Cellular respiration

Test Prep

Choose the letter that best completes the statement or answers the question.

15. Which of the following describes cellular respiration?
   Ⓐ breaks down glucose, produces oxygen
   Ⓑ breaks down glucose, produces carbon dioxide
   Ⓒ breaks down carbon dioxide, produces oxygen
   Ⓓ breaks down carbon dioxide, produces glucose

16. What is inside pollen?
   Ⓕ eggs   Ⓖ ovules
   Ⓗ seeds   Ⓘ sperm

17. A plant with green stems that live only one season is a
   Ⓐ woody plant   Ⓑ conifer
   Ⓒ tuber   Ⓓ herbaceous plant

18. Which of the following plants produces spores that grow into new plants?
   Ⓕ fern   Ⓖ Scotch pine
   Ⓗ peach tree   Ⓘ grass

19. Explain why the answer you chose for Question 18 is best. For each of the answers you did not choose, give a reason why it is not the best choice.

20. **Writing in Science** **Descriptive** Suppose you are going to plant some seeds in your garden. Write a paragraph that describes the conditions you must consider in order for your seeds to germinate.

135

◉ During Reading

As you read the lesson, use the Checkpoint to check your understanding. Some Checkpoints ask you to use the reading target skill.

◉ After Reading

After you have read the chapter, think about what you found out. Exchange ideas with your partner. Compare the list you made before you read the chapter with what you learned by reading it. Answer the questions in the Chapter Review. One question uses the reading target skill.

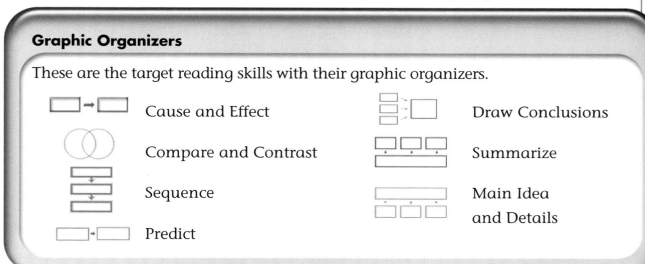

Graphic Organizers

These are the target reading skills with their graphic organizers.

Cause and Effect

Compare and Contrast

Sequence

Predict

Draw Conclusions

Summarize

Main Idea and Details

Science Process Skills

Exploring a Rain Forest

Scientists use process skills when they explore places or investigate events. You will use these skills when you do the activities in this book. Which process skills might scientists use when they explore a tropical rain forest?

Observe

A scientist exploring a rain forest observes many things. You use your senses too to find out about other objects, events, or living things.

Classify

Scientists classify living and nonliving things in a rain forest according to their properties. When you classify, you arrange or sort objects, events, or living things.

Estimate and Measure

Scientists might estimate the size of an organism in a rain forest. When they estimate, they tell what they think an object's size, mass, or temperature will measure. Then they measure these factors in units.

Infer
During an investigation, scientists infer what they think is happening, based on what they already know.

Predict
Before they go into a rain forest, scientists tell what they think they will find.

Make and Use Models
Scientists might make and use models, such as maps, to help plan where to go during an investigation.

Make Operational Definitions
When scientists make operational definitions, they describe objects or events based on their experiences.

Science Process Skills

Form Questions and Hypotheses

Think of a statement that you can test to solve a problem or answer a question about a python or other organism in a tropical rain forest.

Collect Data

Scientists collect data from their observations in rain forests. They put the data into charts or tables.

Interpret Data

Scientists use the information they collected to solve problems or answer questions.

If you were a scientist, you might explore a tropical rain forest or other area. What questions might you have about the things you see? How would you use process skills in your investigation?

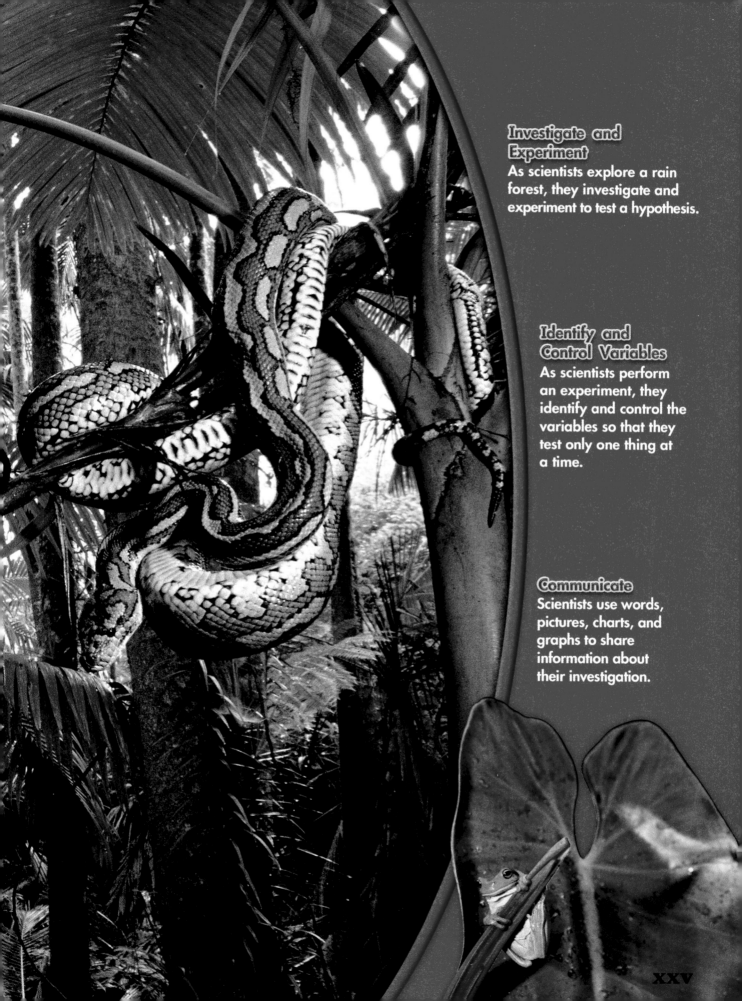

Investigate and Experiment
As scientists explore a rain forest, they investigate and experiment to test a hypothesis.

Identify and Control Variables
As scientists perform an experiment, they identify and control the variables so that they test only one thing at a time.

Communicate
Scientists use words, pictures, charts, and graphs to share information about their investigation.

Using Scientific Methods for Science Inquiry

Scientists use scientific methods as they work. Scientific methods are organized ways to answer questions and solve problems. Scientific methods include the steps shown here. Scientists might not use all the steps. They might not use the steps in this order. You will use scientific methods when you do the **Full Inquiry** activity at the end of each unit. You also will use scientific methods when you do **Science Fair Projects.**

Ask a question.

You might have a question about something you observe.

What material is best for keeping heat in water?

State your hypothesis.

A hypothesis is a possible answer to your question.

If I wrap the jar in fake fur, then the water will stay warmer longer.

Identify and control variables.

Variables are things that can change. For a fair test, you choose just one variable to change. Keep all other variables the same.

Test other materials. Put the same amount of warm water in other jars that are the same size and shape.

Test your hypothesis.

Make a plan to test your hypothesis. Collect materials and tools. Then follow your plan.

Collect and record your data.

Keep good records of what you do and find out. Use tables and pictures to help.

Interpret your data.

Organize your notes and records to make them clear. Make diagrams, charts, or graphs to help.

State your conclusion.

Your conclusion is a decision you make based on your data. Communicate what you found out. Tell whether or not your data supported your hypothesis.

Fake fur did the best job of keeping the water warm.

Go further.

Use what you learn. Think of new questions to test or better ways to do a test.

Ask a
Question

State Your
Hypothesis

Identify
and Control
Variables

Test Your
Hypothesis

Collect
and Record
Your Data

Interpret
Your Data

State Your
Conclusion

Go Further

Science Tools

Scientists use many different kinds of tools. Tools can make objects appear larger. They can help you measure volume, temperature, length, distance, and mass. Tools can help you figure out amounts and analyze your data. Tools can also help you find the latest scientific information.

Graduated cylinders and beakers can be used to measure volume, or the amount of space an object takes up.

A **hand lens** makes objects appear larger. A hand lens, or magnifying glass, doesn't enlarge things as much as a microscope does, but you can easily carry a hand lens.

A **microscope** uses a series of lenses that make objects appear larger. When you change the combination and position of lenses, you magnify objects by different amounts.

A **stopwatch** is a watch with a hand that can be stopped or started. It can be used for timing experiments.

A meterstick or **metric ruler** is used to measure length. A meterstick is one meter long. The stick is divided into smaller units—usually centimeters and millimeters.

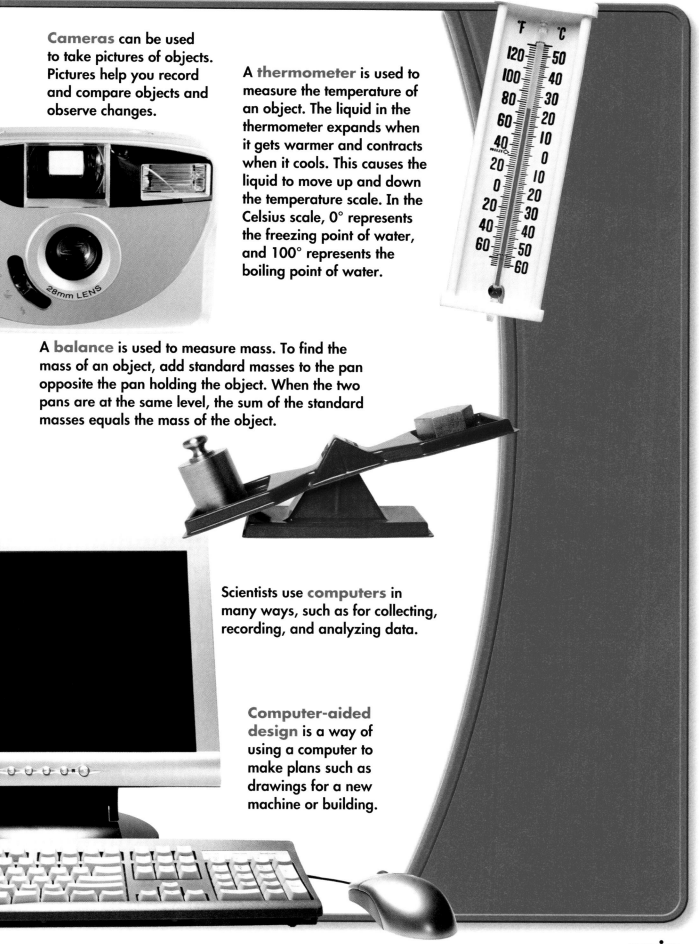

Cameras can be used to take pictures of objects. Pictures help you record and compare objects and observe changes.

A **thermometer** is used to measure the temperature of an object. The liquid in the thermometer expands when it gets warmer and contracts when it cools. This causes the liquid to move up and down the temperature scale. In the Celsius scale, 0° represents the freezing point of water, and 100° represents the boiling point of water.

A **balance** is used to measure mass. To find the mass of an object, add standard masses to the pan opposite the pan holding the object. When the two pans are at the same level, the sum of the standard masses equals the mass of the object.

Scientists use **computers** in many ways, such as for collecting, recording, and analyzing data.

Computer-aided design is a way of using a computer to make plans such as drawings for a new machine or building.

Science Tools

Scientists use **barometers** to measure the air pressure, which can be a good indicator of weather patterns.

Tape recorders are used by scientists to record and learn about sounds made by organisms or objects.

Field guides are books that you might take into the field to learn the details of objects that you are observing, such as plants, animals, or stars.

Calculators make analyzing data easier and faster.

A **spring scale** is used to measure force. Because the weight of an object is a measure of the force of gravity on the object, you can use a spring scale to measure weight in grams.

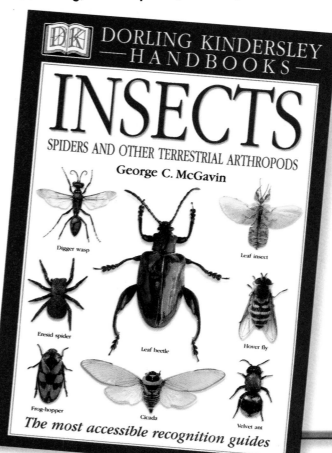

DORLING KINDERSLEY HANDBOOKS

INSECTS

SPIDERS AND OTHER TERRESTRIAL ARTHROPODS

George C. McGavin

Digger wasp

Leaf insect

Eresid spider

Leaf beetle

Hover fly

Frog-hopper

Cicada

Velvet ant

The most accessible recognition guides

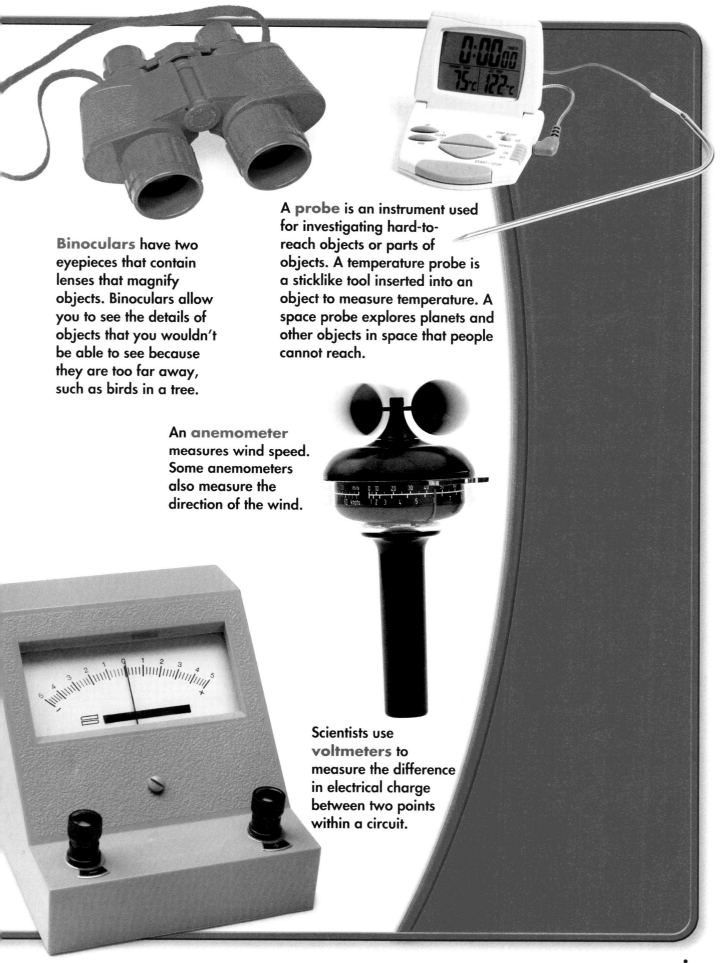

Binoculars have two eyepieces that contain lenses that magnify objects. Binoculars allow you to see the details of objects that you wouldn't be able to see because they are too far away, such as birds in a tree.

A **probe** is an instrument used for investigating hard-to-reach objects or parts of objects. A temperature probe is a sticklike tool inserted into an object to measure temperature. A space probe explores planets and other objects in space that people cannot reach.

An **anemometer** measures wind speed. Some anemometers also measure the direction of the wind.

Scientists use **voltmeters** to measure the difference in electrical charge between two points within a circuit.

Safety in Science

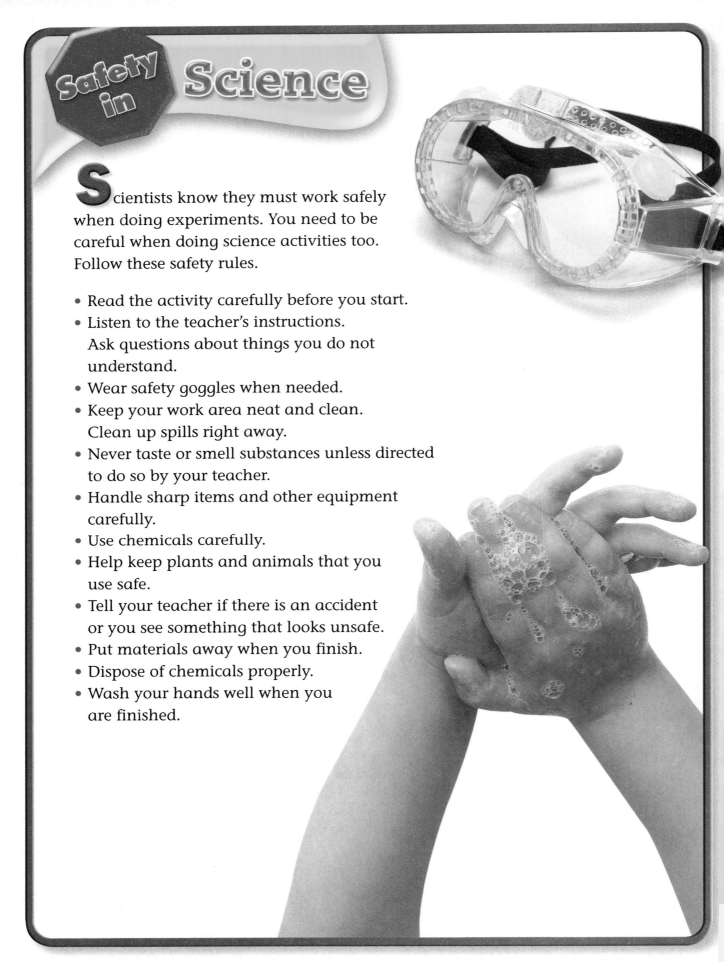

Scientists know they must work safely when doing experiments. You need to be careful when doing science activities too. Follow these safety rules.

- Read the activity carefully before you start.
- Listen to the teacher's instructions. Ask questions about things you do not understand.
- Wear safety goggles when needed.
- Keep your work area neat and clean. Clean up spills right away.
- Never taste or smell substances unless directed to do so by your teacher.
- Handle sharp items and other equipment carefully.
- Use chemicals carefully.
- Help keep plants and animals that you use safe.
- Tell your teacher if there is an accident or you see something that looks unsafe.
- Put materials away when you finish.
- Dispose of chemicals properly.
- Wash your hands well when you are finished.

You Will Discover

- what Earth's Sun and Moon are like.
- what causes the phases of the Moon.
- how Earth-Moon-Sun relationships relate to days, years, and seasons.
- what causes solar and lunar eclipses.

Chapter 19

Earth, Sun, and Moon

online
Student Edition
sfsuccessnet.com

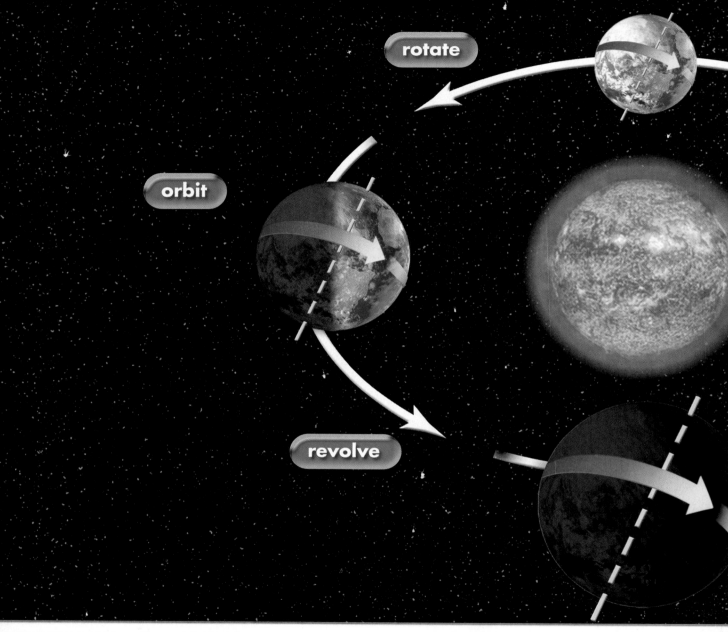

rotate

orbit

revolve

lunar eclipse

530

Chapter 19 Vocabulary

solar eclipse

Explore How can you make a sundial?

A sundial can show one effect of Earth's movement.

Materials

posterboard

drawing compass and modeling clay

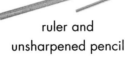

ruler and unsharpened pencil

directional compass and clock

marker

What to Do

1 Draw a 9 inch circle on the posterboard. Mark the center of the circle and draw a line through it. Write *noon* at one end of the line.

2 Place a small mound of clay at the center of the circle. Press the eraser end of a pencil into the clay so the pencil stands upright.

3 Take your sundial and a directional compass outside on a sunny day. Place the sundial so that "noon" on your sundial points north.

noon

N

At noon, the pencil's shadow falls along a line pointing north

4 **Observe** the pencil's shadow moving around the sundial. At each hour, mark the position of the shadow. Mark as many hours as you can.

Explain Your Results

Infer How could you change your sundial to tell Daylight Saving Time?
(Hint: 1 P.M. Standard Time = 2 P.M. Daylight Saving Time)

Process Skills

You can make an **inference** based on your experience and **observations**.

How to Read Science

Main Idea and Details

The **main idea** tells what a paragraph is about. Knowing how to quickly find the main idea of a paragraph can help you understand and remember what you read.

- Sometimes the main idea is not stated. You must **infer** it.

- Look for **details** that give clues to the main idea. Then put together the facts to figure out the main idea.

Science Article

Seeing the Moon

When you look at the Moon at night, it's hard to believe that it doesn't give off its own light. What you see is sunlight bouncing off the Moon. When the Moon is between Earth and the Sun, the back part of the Moon is lit. We can't see that part from Earth. At that time, the part of the Moon facing Earth is dark, so you can't see the Moon when you look at the sky.

Apply It!

Make a graphic organizer like this one. Record **details** from the paragraph. Then write a **main idea** sentence.

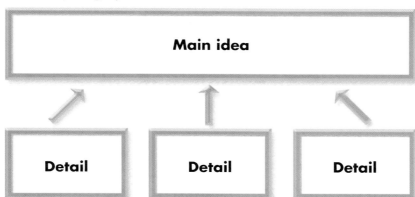

You Are There!

A trip to the Sun wouldn't be much fun! Even the coolest regions are thousands of degrees hotter than Earth. But if you could somehow withstand the intense heat, you would see a swirl of glowing gases. Nearby you might see a tremendous ring of gases thousands of miles high. Huge flares of unimaginably hot gases would suddenly burst out into space above you. What are these huge flares?

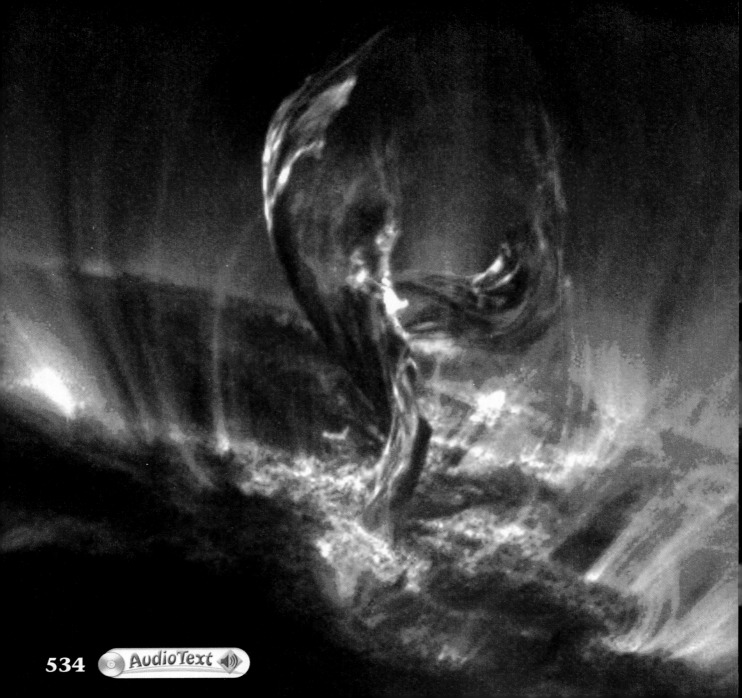

AudioText

What are the characteristics of Earth's Sun and Moon?

The Sun provides Earth with the heat and light needed to sustain life. The Moon revolves around Earth. The Moon's phases are caused by its position relative to Earth and the Sun.

Solar prominence

Our Sun

Our Sun is a star, just like all the stars you see in the night sky. The Sun appears larger only because it is much closer to Earth. The Sun looks like a ball of fire, but it isn't burning at all. The Sun is made of hot gases called plasma. The plasma is so hot that it glows, like the glow of the wire in a light bulb.

The inner part of the Sun is a dense core with a temperature around 15,000,000°C. Reactions among particles in the core release energy, part of which provides light and heat for Earth. Life couldn't exist on Earth without energy from the Sun. Plants use the light energy to produce food for themselves and for other organisms that eat plants. Without the Sun's energy, Earth would be a cold, lifeless rock.

The Sun has no solid surface. Outside the core are swirling layers of plasma. Huge loops of gases, called prominences, extend thousands of kilometers out from the Sun. Some prominences are held in place for weeks. Others explode into space. Intense, temporary releases of energy from the Sun's surface are called solar flares. Energy from these flares sometimes reaches Earth. This energy can cause beautiful light displays called auroras, usually seen near Earth's poles.

1. ✓ **Checkpoint** What causes the light that the Sun produces?
2. ⟳ **Main Idea and Details** Write a main idea statement about the Sun from the paragraphs above. Give details to support your main idea.

Earth's Moon

Looking at the Moon on a clear night, you might think that it shines like the Sun. But the Moon has no light of its own. The light you see is the sunlight that reflects off the Moon's surface. Unlike the Sun with its swirling hot plasma, the Moon is like a giant rock in space. The Moon has almost no atmosphere.

The Moon **rotates,** or spins, on its axis while it revolves around Earth. **Revolve** means to "move on a path around an object." Features of the Moon are easy to spot because its same side always faces Earth. Why do we only see one side? The time for one rotation and one revolution of the Moon are the same as Earth days. Each time the Moon revolves around Earth, it also rotates one time.

Phases of the Moon

If you look at the Moon each night for a month, you'll notice that it seems to change shape. Of course, the Moon doesn't really change shape. The phases of the Moon are the different shapes that the Moon seems to have. The shapes change because the size of the lighted part that we can see from Earth changes. Only the half of the Moon that faces the Sun at any time is lighted. The phases you see depend on the positions of the Moon, Earth, and the Sun.

A new moon is the dark phase of the Moon. During a new moon, the unlighted side of the Moon faces Earth. On nights just after a new moon, the Moon begins to wax. *Waxing* means "gradually growing larger." The Moon is waxing when more of its lighted part can be seen each night. A full moon is the completely lighted phase of the Moon. On nights after a full moon, the Moon begins to wane. *Waning* means "gradually becoming smaller." The Moon is waning when less of its lighted part can be seen each night. The Moon continues to wane until you once again see a new moon, and the cycle continues. A complete cycle of Moon phases occurs about every 29.5 days.

Waxing Crescent

As the Moon begins to wax, a crescent of light begins to show on the side.

First Quarter

As the Moon continues to wax, you can see half of its lighted side.

Astronauts on this *Apollo 16* mission to the Moon in 1972 collected samples, performed experiments, and took photographs.

Waxing Gibbous

The Moon continues to wax. The shape of the Moon we see is now called gibbous.

Full Moon

About two weeks after a new moon, the Moon appears fully lighted. It has completed half its path around Earth.

Waning Gibbous

The Moon begins to wane. The gibbous shape is now on the left side of the Moon.

Third Quarter

The Moon has now traveled about three quarters of its path around Earth. The lighted half you see is now on the side opposite that of the First Quarter.

Waning Crescent

The Moon is now waning. Each night, the lighted portion grows smaller until only a thin crescent of light is visible.

Astronaut Buzz Aldrin took this photo of his boot print in the Moon's soil during the *Apollo 11* mission.

The *Apollo 11* astronauts brought rocks from the Moon back to Earth. Scientists studied microscopic views of the rocks to learn about their properties.

Learning About the Moon

Although the Moon has been known to humans since prehistoric times, the first visit to the Moon by a spacecraft didn't happen until 1957. That year the unmanned Soviet spacecraft *Luna 2* landed on the surface of the Moon. Ten years later, *Apollo 11* astronauts Edwin "Buzz" Aldrin and Neil Armstrong were the first humans to land on the Moon. Their landing was followed by five more Moon landings, the last in 1972.

Scientists study information they collected on those journeys to learn about the Moon, Earth, and the entire solar system. Because the Moon has almost no atmosphere, its surface remains undisturbed. Scientists can study the craters and other features of the Moon's surface to help determine the age of the Moon and of Earth.

✓Lesson Checkpoint

1. Explain why the same side of the Moon always faces Earth. Use the terms *rotate* and *revolve*.

2. **Technology** in Science Space exploration began on October 4, 1957, when the Soviet Union launched *Sputnik 1*. Find out what other spacecraft were launched between that date and the last mission to the Moon in 1972. Draw a time line of those events.

537

What are the effects of the movements of Earth and the Moon?

Days, years, and seasons are caused by Earth's rotation, revolution, and tilt on its axis. The changing positions of the Sun, Moon, and Earth can cause solar and lunar eclipses.

In the evening, the Sun appears to sink below the western horizon.

At midnight, the side of Earth opposite to you experiences the noon Sun.

Earth on its Axis

Think about a time thousands of years ago, before telescopes had been invented and before astronauts had ever traveled into space. What did people think of Earth and its Sun? If you look at the daytime sky, the Sun rises in the east and sets in the west. People naturally thought the Sun was moving around Earth.

We now know that the Sun is the center of our solar system and that Earth and other planets revolve around the Sun. Earth also rotates on its axis, an imaginary line between its poles. A day is the total time for a planet to make one complete rotation. The Sun seems to revolve around Earth because of Earth's rotation.

If you wake up early in the morning, you might see the Sun just beginning to rise above the eastern horizon. The Sun always seems to rise in the east because Earth spins from west to east. Because you spin along with Earth, the Sun is first visible in the east. You experience daytime as long as the Sun is visible from your location on Earth. Daytime ends when Earth has turned enough that the Sun seems to set in the west. Nighttime is when the Sun is no longer visible to you.

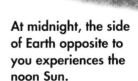

To understand Earth's rotation, picture Earth spinning on a pole. The speed of Earth's rotation at the equator is about 1,670 km/h.

Heat from the Sun is most intense around noon when the Sun is at its highest point.

As the Sun rises in the eastern sky, sunlight begins to warm Earth.

When you wake up on a winter morning, it may still be dark outside. If you wake up at the same time in summer, it may have been light outside for hours. The number of hours of daylight changes throughout the year. Notice on the globe how Earth is tilted on its axis. One half of Earth is usually tilted slightly toward the Sun. That side has more daylight hours and fewer nighttime hours. The other half of Earth has fewer daylight hours and more nighttime hours.

The tilt of Earth's axis has an even greater effect at the poles. When the northern part of Earth is tilted toward the Sun, the Sun never fully sets at the North Pole. The same is true at the South Pole when it is tilted toward the Sun. Daylight and darkness at the poles each last six months.

You may have noticed that the Moon is sometimes visible during the day. The Moon can be seen whenever it is on your side of Earth. This is sometimes during daytime and sometimes during nighttime.

1. ✔Checkpoint Why does the Sun seem to rise in the eastern sky?

2. Math in Science If an object weighs 300 newtons on Earth, about how much would it weigh on the Moon?

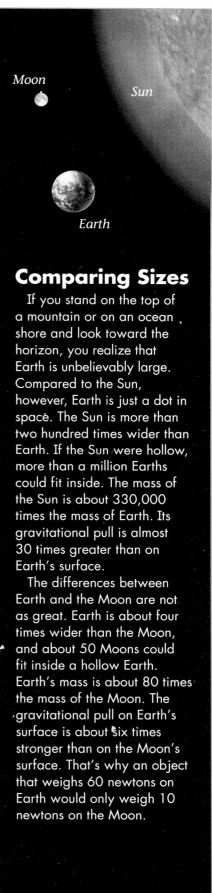

Moon

Sun

Earth

Comparing Sizes

If you stand on the top of a mountain or on an ocean shore and look toward the horizon, you realize that Earth is unbelievably large. Compared to the Sun, however, Earth is just a dot in space. The Sun is more than two hundred times wider than Earth. If the Sun were hollow, more than a million Earths could fit inside. The mass of the Sun is about 330,000 times the mass of Earth. Its gravitational pull is almost 30 times greater than on Earth's surface.

The differences between Earth and the Moon are not as great. Earth is about four times wider than the Moon, and about 50 Moons could fit inside a hollow Earth. Earth's mass is about 80 times the mass of the Moon. The gravitational pull on Earth's surface is about six times stronger than on the Moon's surface. That's why an object that weighs 60 newtons on Earth would only weigh 10 newtons on the Moon.

Earth's Orbit and Seasons

Like all objects in space, Earth tends to move in a straight line. The force of the Sun's gravity, however, pulls Earth toward the Sun out of a straight-line path. As a result, Earth revolves around the Sun. An **orbit** is the path of an object that revolves around another object. Earth's orbit around the Sun is an ellipse, a slightly flattened circle. A year, about 365 days, is the total amount of time Earth takes to make one orbit around the Sun.

Because Earth's orbit is an ellipse, it is sometimes slightly closer to the Sun than at other times. People often think summer is when Earth is closer to the Sun, but is this really true? To answer this question, think about standing close to a heater so that your face feels warm. If you step just a few centimeters back, the warmth you feel doesn't change. If you turn around, however, your face no longer feels warm.

In a similar way, the slight difference in the distance to the Sun as Earth moves around its orbit has no effect on seasons. In fact, Earth is slightly closer to the Sun when the northern half experiences winter. Earth's tilt on its axis is what causes seasons. The Sun warms the side of Earth that tilts toward it more than it does the side tilted away. When the North Pole tilts toward the Sun, the northern half of Earth has summer and the southern half has winter. When the South Pole tilts toward the Sun, the seasons are reversed. In spring and in fall, neither pole tilts toward the Sun. Both the northern and southern halves of Earth have mild temperatures.

The tilt of Earth's axis affects how directly the Sun shines on Earth as it travels in its orbit.

The North Pole tilts away from the Sun. The Sun's rays are very spread out here. The Northern Hemisphere receives the least amount of energy at this time of year. Temperatures drop, and winter sets in.

The Sun's rays strike the Earth more directly near the equator. The rays are concentrated, not spread out. Concentrated energy gives this region warm summer weather.

In summer, the Sun's rays point almost directly toward you at noon. The direct sunlight makes the days very warm. The shadow you make is very small. As each day passes, the Sun's rays strike you at a greater and greater angle—we say the Sun is lower in the sky. With less direct rays from the Sun, the days are not as warm. Your noontime shadow gets longer and longer. You have winter when the part of Earth where you live is tilted away from the Sun. At noon, the angle of the Sun's rays is large, and you make a long shadow. A year can be defined as the time between the days when your shadow is at its shortest.

1. **✓ Checkpoint** How does your noontime shadow change throughout the year?
2. **Writing in Science** **Descriptive** Write a paragraph describing seasons if Earth were not tilted on its axis.

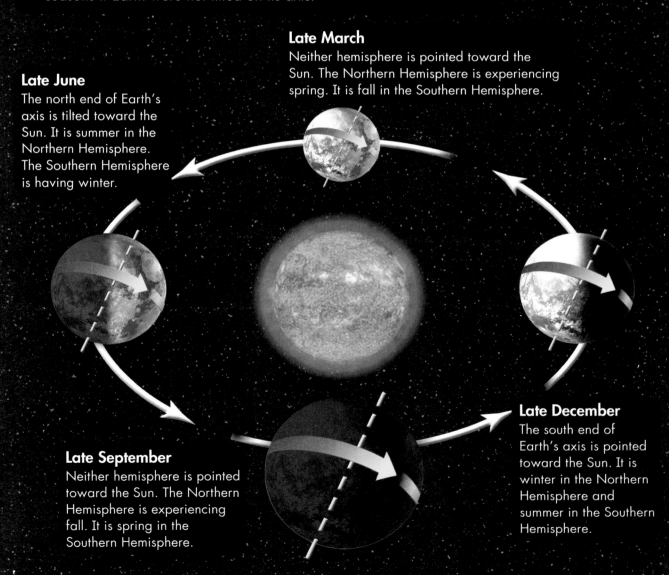

Late March
Neither hemisphere is pointed toward the Sun. The Northern Hemisphere is experiencing spring. It is fall in the Southern Hemisphere.

Late June
The north end of Earth's axis is tilted toward the Sun. It is summer in the Northern Hemisphere. The Southern Hemisphere is having winter.

Late December
The south end of Earth's axis is pointed toward the Sun. It is winter in the Northern Hemisphere and summer in the Southern Hemisphere.

Late September
Neither hemisphere is pointed toward the Sun. The Northern Hemisphere is experiencing fall. It is spring in the Southern Hemisphere.

Solar Eclipses

If you draw a picture of Earth's orbit around the Sun on a piece of paper, you can't draw the Moon's true orbit around Earth on the same paper. The Moon's orbit is tilted slightly at an angle from Earth's orbit. You can see the effect of this during a new moon. If the new moon occurs in daytime, you can see the Sun. The Moon is a little above or below the Sun because of the tilt of its orbit. Sometimes, however, the orbit of the Moon crosses exactly between the Sun and Earth. The Moon eclipses, or covers, the Sun. A **solar eclipse** occurs when the Moon blocks the light of the Sun.

The Moon makes two types of shadows on Earth during an eclipse. The umbra is the darker, inner part of an eclipse shadow. The penumbra is the lighter, outer part of an eclipse shadow. You can see these on the picture at the right. Even though solar eclipses occur several times a year, each place on Earth only experiences one every few hundred years.

During a solar eclipse, a place on Earth may experience a total or partial eclipse of the Sun or no eclipse at all. A total eclipse is when the umbra passes over an area. For several minutes, the Sun is completely blocked from view. The sky darkens, and the stars are visible in daytime. Because the Moon's shadow is so small, only a small part of Earth experiences a total eclipse. Nearby areas that are in the penumbra experience a partial eclipse. A partial eclipse can also occur when the umbra completely misses Earth and only the penumbra passes over.

It's important to remember that you should never look directly at the Sun. A good way to view an eclipse is by using two pieces of white cardboard. Place one piece of cardboard on the ground. Place a pinhole in the center of the other piece. Point the pinhole at the Sun so that you see a round image on the other cardboard. The round spot of light you see on the paper is a pinhole image of the Sun.

Time-lapse photo of a lunar eclipse

Lunar Eclipses

A different kind of eclipse can occur during a full moon, when Earth is between the Sun and the Moon. A **lunar eclipse** happens when the Moon passes through Earth's shadow. You can safely watch a lunar eclipse. During a total eclipse, you might see the Moon passing through Earth's shadow for almost two hours. The time is shorter for partial eclipses. Unlike a solar eclipse, a lunar eclipse can be seen by most parts of Earth where it is nighttime. Lunar and solar eclipses occur about twice a year, but because lunar eclipses are visible from half the Earth, you are much more likely to see one.

Total Solar Eclipse

Umbra

Penumbra

Lunar Eclipse

✔ **Lesson Checkpoint**

1. What are two ways an area can experience a partial eclipse?

2. ↻ **Main Idea and Details** Write details to support this main idea: During a solar eclipse, the Moon blocks the light of the Sun.

3. **Writing** in Science **Expository** During a total lunar eclipse, the Moon appears slightly red. Research to find the cause of this effect and write a paragraph explaining it.

Investigate How can you make a spectroscope?

Different colors of light are given off by different materials. By studying the light from the Sun, scientists can learn about the materials that make up the Sun. Scientists use a spectroscope to separate light into its different colors. In this activity you will make a spectroscope and compare the color pattern made by "white" light from 3 different sources.

Materials

compact disc

cardboard tube with viewing hole and slit

cardboard circle with slit

masking tape

assorted light sources

Process Skills

You can make an **inference** based on your **observations** of the spectra of assorted light sources.

What to Do

1 Tape the cardboard circle to one end of the tube.

2 Slide a CD into the slot above the viewing hole. Point the slit at a light source and look through the viewing hole. Look for bands of color.

3 Record your **observations.**

Light Source	Spectroscope Image	Description or Drawing
Fluorescent ceiling light		
Compact fluorescent light bulb		
Incandescent light bulb		

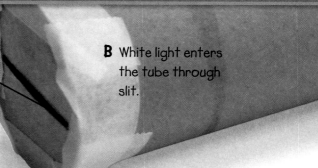
A Point the slit at the light source.
B White light enters the tube through slit.

Explain Your Results

1. What did you **observe** when you looked through the viewing hole?

2. Compare and contrast the spectrum from the incandescent light bulb and the spectrum from the fluorescent ceiling light.

3. **Infer** How might a scientist use information about sunlight to learn about the Sun?

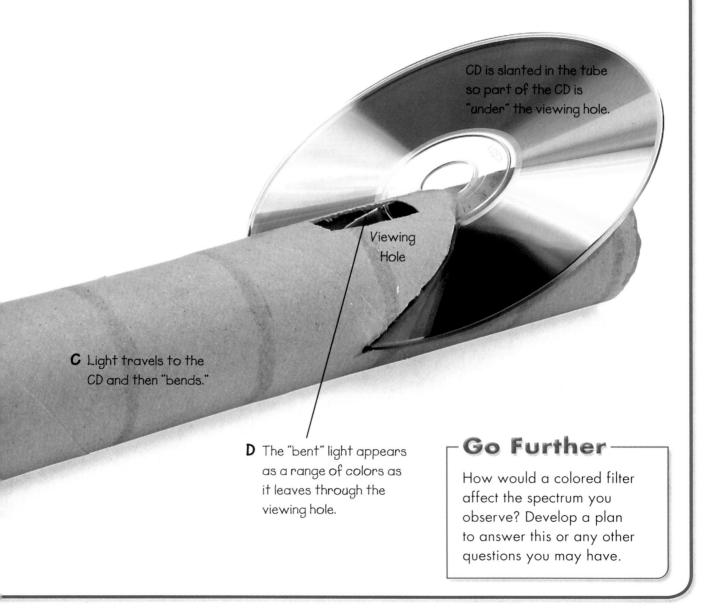

CD is slanted in the tube so part of the CD is "under" the viewing hole.

Viewing Hole

C Light travels to the CD and then "bends."

D The "bent" light appears as a range of colors as it leaves through the viewing hole.

Go Further

How would a colored filter affect the spectrum you observe? Develop a plan to answer this or any other questions you may have.

Math in Science

SPEED in Space

Objects in space travel great distances at speeds much faster than humans travel on Earth. The Moon travels around the Earth at a speed of about 3700 kilometers per hour!

One of the world's fastest runners set a record in a 100 meter race with an average speed of 10.2 meters per second. Compare this speed with the speed of the Moon given above.

Speed is one type of rate. To compare rates, it is usually necessary to express them using the same units. One way to do this is to analyze the units used for one of the rates and use them to divide and simplify the rate.

To change 10.2 m/s to km/h, first change 10.2 m to km.

$$10.2 \text{ m} \div \frac{1000 \text{ m}}{1 \text{ km}} = \frac{10.2 \text{ m}}{1} \times \frac{1 \text{ km}}{1000 \text{ m}} = \frac{10.2 \text{ km}}{1000} = 0.0102 \text{ km}$$

$$\frac{0.0102 \text{ km}}{1 \text{ s}} \times \frac{60 \text{ s}}{1 \text{ min}} \times \frac{60 \text{ min}}{1 \text{ h}} = \frac{0.0102 \text{ km} \times 60 \times 60}{1 \text{ h}} = 36.72 \text{ km/h}$$

Running 36.72 km/h is very fast for a human, but the Moon travels more than 100 times as fast!

Use the information on page 546 to answer each question.

1. Earth travels around the Sun at a speed of 30,000 meters per second. Express this speed in kilometers per hour.

2. As Earth rotates on its axis, a point on the equator is traveling at 1,674 kilometers per hour. Express this speed in meters per second. Round your answer to the nearest meter.

3. The Moon makes one revolution around Earth in about 27 days and 7 hours. About how far does the Moon travel in that time?

4. The average distance from Earth to the Moon is 384,400 km. If you could travel to the Moon—a distance of about 384,400 km—at highway speeds, about how many weeks would it take? The speed limit on many American highways is about 100 km/h.

Lab zone Take-Home Activity

Use library resources to research the Apollo space missions to the Moon. Then write a story about traveling to the Moon yourself. Include your average speed, traveling time, and length of stay on the Moon.

Use Vocabulary

lunar eclipse (p. 542)	**rotates** (p. 536)
orbit (p. 540)	**solar eclipse** (p. 542)
revolve (p. 536)	

Use the vocabulary term from above that best completes each sentence.

1. The Moon _____ on its axis.

2. The _____ of Earth is its path around the Sun.

3. A(n) _____ occurs when the Moon completely blocks out the Sun's light.

4. The time for Earth to _____ around the Sun once is a year.

5. A(n) _____ occurs when the Moon passes through Earth's shadow.

Explain Concepts

6. Why are you more likely to see a lunar eclipse than a solar eclipse?

7. How does Earth's motion relate to a day and a year?

8. What causes seasons?

9. Explain why your shadow is shorter in summer than in winter.

10. Create a drawing to explain the phases of the Moon.

Process Skills

11. **Infer** Why are scientists able to predict when solar and lunar eclipses occur?

12. **Model** Make a model that shows how Earth revolves around the Sun.

13. **Predict** The picture shows the setup for an experiment to see how the angle of light hitting a surface affects temperature. Which thermometer on the globe do you predict will have a higher temperature? Why?

Main Idea and Details

14. Make a graphic organizer like the one below for each lesson in this chapter. Fill in the main idea and supporting details for each lesson.

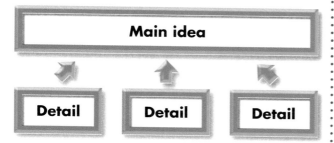

Main idea

Detail **Detail** **Detail**

Test Prep

Choose the letter that best completes the statement or answers the question.

15. Which of the following is a reasonable time that a total solar eclipse might take?
- Ⓐ 5 minutes
- Ⓑ 30 minutes
- Ⓒ 1 hour
- Ⓓ 2 hours

16. Which phase can you see when the Moon is waning?
- Ⓕ first quarter moon
- Ⓖ half moon
- Ⓗ new moon
- Ⓘ third quarter moon

17. During which season is the part of Earth where you live tilted toward the Sun?
- Ⓐ fall
- Ⓑ spring
- Ⓒ summer
- Ⓓ winter

18. The Sun is made up of
- Ⓕ solid rock.
- Ⓖ auroras.
- Ⓗ liquids.
- Ⓘ plasma.

19. Explain why the answer you chose for Question 16 is best. For each of the answers you did not choose, give a reason why it is not the best choice.

20. Writing in Science **Narrative** Write a journal entry about a visit to the Sun. Explain what you see and feel on your visit. Remember to include what you see as you look from the Sun and the sky.

Reducing Drag to Save Fuel

When you think about NASA, you probably think of space travel and exploration. However, the work of some NASA scientists has helped improve travel right here on Earth. For example, the shape of some trucks you see on the road has been influenced by NASA technologies.

Until the 1970s, truck cabs were shaped like boxes with sharp corners. These sharp-cornered trucks would pass a NASA aerospace engineer as he rode his bike to and from work every day. The speed and shape of the trucks resulted in very strong and uneven wind gusts that pushed the scientist and his bike toward the side of the road. After the trucks passed, he would get pulled back toward the road. He realized that the forces pushing and pulling him could be costing the truck drivers money—they made the trucks use more fuel.

The force that the scientist experienced was partly the result of drag, a force that works against the motion of moving objects. A truck must use energy to overcome drag. A truck with a box-shaped cab uses a lot of fuel to overcome drag.

Compare NASA's experimental truck cab with the new cab design.

The scientist decided to help trucks glide through air instead of push through it. In the process, the trucks would encounter less drag and become more fuel-efficient. NASA researchers were working on the effects of drag and wind resistance on different kinds of aircraft and the space shuttle. They applied this knowledge to the design of large trucks. The researchers changed the box-shaped cab of the truck by rounding out its corners and edges. Then they observed the changes in drag. Trucks with the new cab design used much less fuel. This new design is now widely used.

Lab zone Take-Home Activity

How would you design a truck's trailer? Trailers still have a box shape for the purpose of storing cargo. Draw a trailer that would limit the force of drag. Write a paragraph that explains your design.

Astronomer

Is there life on other planets? Are there any planets like Earth in distant solar systems? What are particles of the Sun like? What are the farthest objects we can see in space? What lies beyond that?

These are just a few of the many questions that astronomers try to answer. Astronomers use telescopes, computers, space probes, and other complex instruments to explore the universe.

Most astronomers specialize in a certain area of astronomy. For instance, a cosmologist studies how the universe began. A planetologist is most interested in the planets. Some astronomers are experts in how comets and other objects move in space.

Many astronomers teach at universities. Some work for NASA. Still others work at planetariums and help children and adults alike enjoy the wonders of space. In fact, a lot of people use their own telescopes to explore the night sky on a regular basis. These amateur astronomers have made many important discoveries. Becoming a professional astronomer, however, requires a lot of hard work. Math and science, especially physics, are important subjects to study in high school and college.

Lab zone Take-Home Activity

What stars and planets can be seen in your area right now? Find out by looking at the latest issue of astronomy magazines at the library. Then see how many of these objects you can find in the night sky.

Chapter 20

The Universe

You Will Discover

- what Earth's place is in the universe.
- what the parts of our solar system are.
- why planets differ.
- how stars are born, age, and die.
- how scientists measure distances in space.

online
Student Edition
sfsuccessnet.com

Discovery Channel School
Student DVD

Web Games
Take It to the Net
sfsuccessnet.com

What is Earth's place in the universe?

galaxy

solar system

astronomical unit

Chapter 20 Vocabulary

constellation

light-year

star

magnitude

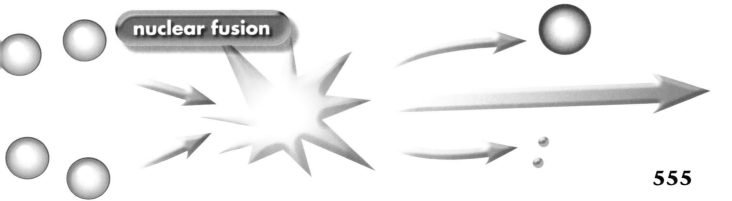

nuclear fusion

Explore How can you find a planet?

In the night sky, both stars and planets can look like points of light. Planets, however, change position or move relative to the stars.

Materials

Sky Pictures

metric ruler

white colored pencil

hand lens

What to Do

1 Look carefully at Sky Picture 1. Which point of light do you think might be the planet Mars?

2 Carefully **observe** Sky Picture 2. Compare it to Sky Picture 1.

3 To help compare the sky pictures, divide each picture into small squares. Then compare the images in corresponding squares one by one.

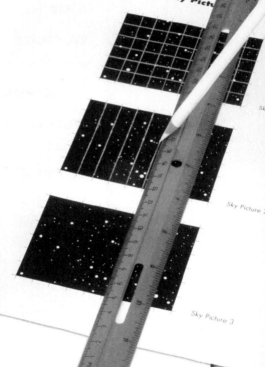

Sky Picture 2

Sky Picture 3

4 Look closely at Sky Picture 3. Compare it to the other two sky pictures.

Explain Your Results

1. How did drawing the grid help you **observe** and compare the 3 pictures?

2. **Infer** Which point of light in the sky pictures do you think is a planet? Explain.

Process Skills

Comparing and contrasting a sequence of sky pictures is one way to carefully **observe** the night sky.

How to Read Science

 Draw Conclusions

When you read, you may form questions that aren't directly answered in the reading passage. In those cases, you often can **infer** ideas from the facts. Then use the facts and your inference to answer the questions by **drawing conclusions.** When you draw a conclusion, you put together facts and ideas to come up with a new idea.

- First, list all the facts.

- Think of a reasonable explanation for the facts.

- Eliminate any conclusions that all the facts do not support.

Read the article below. Look for facts in the article.

Science Article

Seeing the Past

At night when you look at the twinkling stars, the light you see may have taken thousands of years to reach you. The star closest to our Sun is Proxima Centauri. Light given off by this star must travel more than four years to reach Earth. When you look at this star, you are seeing events that took place in the past. How long ago did those events take place?

Apply It!

Make a graphic organizer like this one. List the facts from the science article in your graphic organizer. Write a **conclusion** to answer the question.

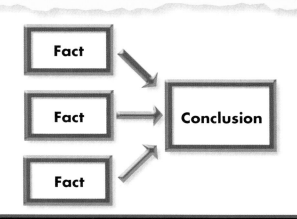

◈ You Are There!

On a camping trip, you go outside after dark and look up at the sky. Amazing! Instead of the misty scattering of light visible in the city, you see glowing balls of fire in every corner. The Big Dipper looks as though you could grasp the handle and pull it down to Earth. What are these brightly gleaming bodies of light in the sky?

Lesson 1

What is Earth's place in the universe?

The universe contains countless billions of stars grouped in galaxies. One of those stars is our Sun. The Sun and all the planets and other bodies around it make up our solar system.

The Universe

Astronomy—the study of space and the objects in it—is one of the oldest sciences. As far back as 3500 B.C. or more, people have been studying the sky. But it wasn't until 1609 when the Italian scientist Galileo first used a crude telescope to study the sky that scientists could see much more than small dots of light in the sky. His findings changed the way people think about space.

Today scientists use powerful telescopes to look into the universe. Scientists aren't sure how far the universe extends, but each year they can see deeper into space. They can study all the energy and matter, as well as the empty space, that make up the universe.

We now know that Earth is part of the Milky Way Galaxy. A **galaxy** is a huge grouping of stars. The universe is made up of clusters of billions of galaxies. Each galaxy is made up of billions of stars.

You may have seen part of the Milky Way Galaxy in the night sky. It looks like a pale white stripe or band across the sky. If you were outside of the Milky Way Galaxy and far away from it, you would see that it is shaped like a flat pinwheel. This type of galaxy is called a spiral galaxy. Our Sun, one of the stars in the Milky Way, is in one of the "arms" of the pinwheel. It is just one of at least 100 billion stars in the Milky Way Galaxy. It appears brighter than other stars because it is much closer to Earth.

Spiral galaxies are just one of the three major types of galaxies. Elliptical galaxies are shaped like an oval, or ellipse. Irregular galaxies do not have a regular shape.

The top photo shows the Milky Way Galaxy. Below you can see a closer view of the stars and dust in the center of the galaxy.

1. ✔Checkpoint To what galaxy does our solar system belong? What type of galaxy is it?

2. Technology in Science Research the major telescopes scientists use today to study the universe. Organize your information into a chart with these headings: Name of telescope, Location, Description, Year developed.

The Planets

The Sun and the cluster of bodies around it make up our **solar system.**
Nine known planets, including Earth, orbit the Sun in our solar system.
In 2005, scientists announced the discovery of what might be the tenth
planet in our solar system. The object will not be given a name until it is
decided whether or not it is a planet. You can see the planets below in the
order they orbit the Sun. All the planets, except Pluto and Mercury, have
orbits that are almost circular. Gravity keeps planets orbiting the Sun.
Some planets have one or more moons. A moon is a natural body that
orbits a planet. Only Mercury and Venus do not have moons.

More than 100,000 asteroids—small bodies made of rock and metal—
also orbit the Sun in our solar system. Comets, which are small icy bodies,
orbit the Sun too. Their orbits are long, narrow ellipses. The far end of a
comet's orbit is deep in space. In part of its orbit, a comet may pass near
the Sun. Then the comet heats up, forming a stream of gas and dust that
trails the comet as it orbits the Sun.

All these objects in our solar system are separated by huge distances.
For that reason, scientists often express distances in our solar system in
astronomical units (AU). An AU is the average distance of Earth from
the Sun—about 149.6 million kilometers.

Mercury
Rocky with craters formed
by meteorites. Extreme
temperatures. Traces of
hydrogen and helium in
atmosphere.

Mars
Covered with red dust. White polar
caps change with seasons. Craters
in southern part. Atmosphere mostly
carbon dioxide. Strong winds blow
red surface dust to create pink sky.

Jupiter
Covered by liquid
hydrogen. Very cold.
Mostly hydrogen with
clouds of ammonia
crystals in atmosphere.

Venus
Mostly rock with craters. Some
volcanoes may be active. Very
hot. Atmosphere made mostly
of carbon dioxide with clouds
of sulfuric acid.

Earth
Mostly water-covered.
Only known planet
with an atmosphere
to support life.

The Inner Planets

	Mercury	Venus	Earth	Mars
Diameter (km)	4,879	12,104	12,756	6,794
Mass (compared to Earth)	0.055	0.82	1.0	0.107
Average distance from the Sun (AU)	0.39	0.72	1	1.52
Time of 1 rotation (Earth days)	58.7	243	1	24.6
Time for 1 revolution (Earth days)	88 days	224.7 days	365.2 days	687 days

The Outer Planets

	Jupiter	Saturn	Uranus	Neptune	Pluto
Diameter (km)	142,984	120,536	51,118	49,528	2,390
Mass (compared to Earth)	318	95	14.5	17.1	0.002
Average distance from Sun (AU)	5.2	9.58	19.20	30.05	39.24
Time of 1 rotation (Earth hours/days)	9.9 hours	10.7 hours	17.2 hours	16.1 hours	6.4 days
Time for 1 revolution (Earth years)	11.9 years	29.4 years	83.7 years	163.7 years	248.0 years

Saturn
Core of rock and iron surrounded by ice and liquid hydrogen. Very cold. Strong winds and swirling clouds of ammonia in atmosphere.

1. **✓ Checkpoint** How do comets and asteroids differ? How are they alike?

2. **⟳ Draw Conclusions** Does the size of a planet affect the time it takes for one revolution around the Sun? Use the facts in the charts to support your answer.

Neptune
Possibly covered by liquid hydrogen and helium. Mostly hydrogen, helium, and methane gases in atmosphere. Appears pale blue.

Uranus
Composed mostly of hydrogen, helium, and methane gases. Very cold. Appears green.

Pluto
Frozen methane and ice. Small amounts of methane gas. Ice cap at North Pole.

A Model of the Solar System

If you took the information about the planets and made a model, it would look something like the one below. The model shows the correct arrangement of planets, but it does not show the relative distances between planets.

The solar system covers very vast distances. On a regular sheet of paper, it would be difficult or impossible to make a drawing of the solar system to scale. The table shows the relative size of and distances between planets if Earth were one millimeter wide at its equator. You can see why showing the planets to scale in this book would be impossible, even if Earth were shrunk to a millimeter.

The Solar System: Relative Distances

	Planet	Size (mm)	Distance from Sun (m)
A	Mercury	0.4	4.5
B	Venus	1.0	8.5
C	Earth	1.0	11.7
D	Mars	0.5	17.9
E	Jupiter	11.2	61
F	Saturn	9.5	112
G	Uranus	4.0	225
H	Neptune	3.9	352
I	Pluto	0.2	459

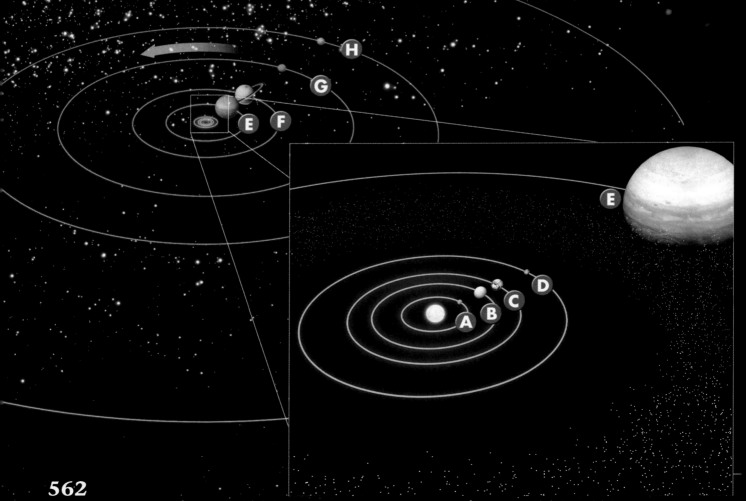

Mars

Venus

Why Planets Differ

You might think that a planet's distance from the Sun is mostly responsible for its characteristics. It's true that a planet close to the Sun receives more warming sunlight than planets farther out. For example, Mars is about twice as far from the Sun as is Venus. This difference is one reason that temperatures on Venus are warmer than on Mars. But distance is only one reason why planets differ. Other factors also help make each planet unique. Let's look at Venus, Earth, and Mars. These planets were similar when they formed billions of years ago, but they have changed in different ways.

A planet's size affects how strong gravity is at its surface. Larger planets have stronger forces of gravity than smaller planets. Strong gravity holds more gases close to the planet, creating a thicker atmosphere. The gravitational force at the surface of Mars is much less than that on Earth or Venus. Its atmosphere is thin with 200 times less gas than Earth's atmosphere. The thin atmosphere holds in less heat, making Mars even colder than it would otherwise be.

Before planetary space probes began in the 1960s, many people thought that Venus might be very much like Earth. It is about the same size and mass as our planet, and its orbit around the Sun is closer to ours than that of any other planet. However, spacecraft have shown that temperatures there reach 475° C, and atmospheric pressure is about 100 times that of Earth.

Why is Venus so different from Earth? Thick clouds cover Venus, and the planet's atmosphere is mostly carbon dioxide. This gas absorbs heat and reflects it back to the planet's surface.

✓ Lesson Checkpoint

1. What is an astronomical unit? Why do scientists use this unit to measure distances in the solar system?
2. List the planets in order from the Sun.
3. **Writing** in Science **Expository** Choose a planet. Find the latest information that scientists have learned about it. Share the information in the form of a newspaper article.

Lesson 2

What do we know about stars?

Hydrogen

Fusion

Small particles

Helium

Energy

Through millions or billions of years, stars produce light and other forms of energy in nuclear fusion reactions. In time, stars run out of fuel and experience enormous changes.

What Stars Are

The twinkling bits of light you see in the night sky tell you little about the activity that goes on in each star. A **star** is a huge, hot, glowing ball of gas. Stars shine because processes that go on in them produce huge amounts of energy. The extremely high temperatures and pressure in the center of a star cause the nuclei of atoms there to bump into each other at incredible speeds. Sometimes two nuclei join to form a single, larger nucleus. This process is called **nuclear fusion.** In most stars, hydrogen nuclei join to form helium nuclei during fusion. Large amounts of energy are given off as radiation, some of which is the light we see.

Distances of Stars

Distances in space are enormous—far too large to use the units we use every day to measure distances, such as kilometers. Even the astronomical unit that is used to measure distances in the solar system is too small. When measuring distances in space, scientists use the light-year. A **light-year** is the distance light travels in one year—9 trillion 460 billion kilometers. Light can travel around Earth seven times in one second!

The Sun is the closest star in our galaxy. The next closest star is Proxima Centauri. It is 4.3 light years away. If the star exploded tonight, you wouldn't see the flash for more than four years! Other galaxies and their stars can be millions of light years away. The light you see from them was given off millions of years ago. You are looking back in time!

SciLinks Take It to the Net
sfsuccessnet.com

keyword: nuclear fusion
code: g6p564

Star Brightness

Imagine the sky as you might see it on a very clear night. A few brightly glowing stars would probably attract your attention right away. You'd have to look more carefully to see fainter stars. Some stars appear bright to us because they are much closer than other stars. These "bright" stars are not necessarily bigger or hotter, however.

Scientists use the term **magnitude** to describe a star's brightness. The brightness we see on Earth is called apparent magnitude. The brightest star we see from Earth is our Sun. No other star has a greater apparent magnitude. In other words, no other star appears brighter.

Scientists have a more accurate measure of a star's true magnitude. Absolute magnitude is the measure of how bright the stars would appear if every star were exactly the same distance from Earth. Scientists use a star's apparent magnitude and its distance from Earth to determine its absolute magnitude. The absolute magnitude of our Sun is 4.8. Other stars may be as much as 156,250 times as bright as the Sun.

Star Color	Temperature	Example Star
Blue	10,000–50,000° C	Bellatrix
White	7,200–9,500° C	Vega
Yellow	5,300–7,000° C	Sun
Red	2,000–5,200° C)	Betelgeuse

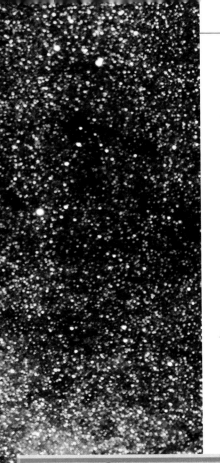

Star Color

If you have ever looked carefully at the night sky, especially through a telescope, you know that some stars appear to be blue, others white, some yellow, and a few red. The color of a star depends on its surface temperature. Think about heating a steel bar. At first, the bar glows red. As it gets hotter, its color changes to orange, yellow, white, and then blue. In the same way, the hottest stars are blue. The coolest stars are red. The chart shows how star color and temperature are related.

How many star colors can you find in this sky picture?

1. ✓Checkpoint What does visible color tell you about a star?
2. Math in Science If a star is 4.6 light-years away from Earth, how far is it in kilometers?

Star Life Cycle

Although stars shine for billions of years, they do not live forever. Like living organisms, stars change as they get older and eventually die. The temperature, size, color, and brightness of a star change as it goes through different stages of its life cycle.

A star is born inside a nebula, a huge cloud of hydrogen and other gases in space. Gravity pulls the gas particles within a nebula together. As the clump attracts more and more particles, it heats up. Nuclear fusion begins when the star's core reaches about 10,000,000°C. The energy produced during fusion heats the gases, which push outward as gravity pulls inward. Eventually, the push of gases becomes greater than the pull of gravity. Energy from fusion reaches the star's surface, and a star is born. Follow the diagram to see how a star changes during its life cycle.

Red Giant
When a star has used up most of its hydrogen, nuclear fusion slows. The outward pressure of hot gases no longer balances the inward pull of gravity. The star begins to collapse. The rising temperature caused by the rising pressure causes helium atoms to collide and fuse into larger nuclei, such as a carbon nucleus. Outer layers of the star expand and turn red as they cool somewhat. Our Sun will probably become a red giant in this way about 5 billion years from now.

Mid-sized Stars
A small or mid-sized star such as our Sun glows yellow for about 10 billion years.

Nebula
Huge clouds of gases and dust form in space.

Massive Stars
A star that is 10 to 30 times more massive than the Sun spends most of its life as a blue star. It glows blue for about 1 to 20 million years.

Nova

Many stars are paired with a partner star. These systems are called binary (two) stars. If one star is a white dwarf, its gravity attracts gases from the partner star. If enough hot gases collect around the dwarf, it may explode, shining so brightly that to viewers on Earth it looks like a new star. This event is called a nova, from the Latin word for "new."

Black Dwarf

A black dwarf is a dead star. It is still a compact, dense body, but because it has used up all its fuel, it does not shine.

White Dwarf

A red giant gradually loses its outer, gaseous layers into space. What is left is a very hot, dense, compact core known as a white dwarf.

Supernova

After a time, gravity pulls the outer parts of a supergiant toward the dense center. Pressure and temperature increase so much that the star explodes, producing a brilliant supernova. What is left behind becomes a neutron star or, rarely, a black hole.

Supergiant

A supergiant is like a red giant, but on a much bigger scale. Nuclear fusion in the core of a red supergiant creates heavier elements, such as iron. The outer layers expand tremendously, becoming cooler and redder.

1. **✓ Checkpoint** What happens to a star when it first begins to run out of fuel?

2. **Social Studies in Science** The Crab Nebula was first seen in China in 1054. Find out more about this supernova and what scientists have learned about it since then. Make a time line of your information.

Constellations

You may have heard people refer to groups of stars with names such as Orion, Leo, Scorpius, and Gemini. These names were first given to groups of stars by the ancient Greeks. The Greeks associated the star patterns with their myths or gods. They named 48 of these star groups, called **constellations.** For example, in Greek mythology, Orion was a handsome hunter who fell in love with the goddess Artemis. Artemis placed Orion in the night sky after accidentally killing him.

Today scientists divide the sky into 88 constellations. Every star is part of a constellation, but stars within a constellation are not necessarily related in any other way.

One of the best-known constellations today is Ursa Major, which means "big bear." The star group called the Big Dipper, which you might be familiar with, is part of Ursa Major. The two stars at the end of the bowl of the Big Dipper always point at the North Star, which is always directly over the North Pole.

If you were able to see both the Sun and stars at the same time, you would notice that the Sun seems to pass through the same ring of constellations each year. The relative position of Earth and the Sun determines where the Sun appears to be among the constellations. This band of stars in which the Sun appears to move is known as the zodiac. Find the zodiac in the picture. How many constellations do you recognize?

The constellation Orion

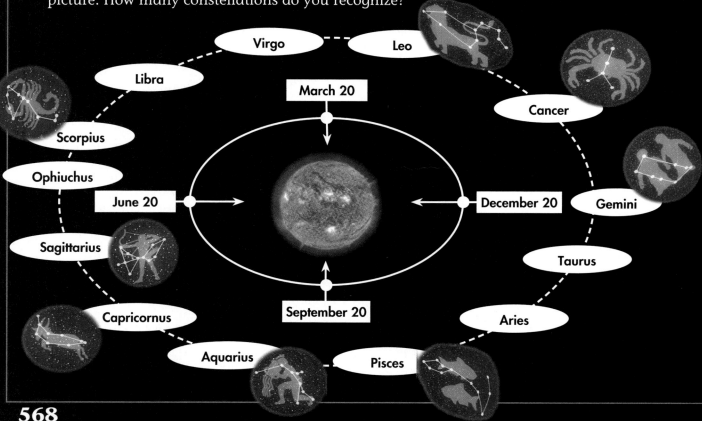

Virgo · Leo · Libra · March 20 · Cancer · Scorpius · Cancer · Ophiuchus · June 20 · December 20 · Gemini · Sagittarius · Taurus · Capricornus · September 20 · Aries · Aquarius · Pisces

Earth spins from west to east on its axis. This movement makes stars appear to move in the opposite direction.

Constellation Movement

If you are a star watcher, you know that the pattern of the nighttime sky changes from hour to hour. A starry sky looks different early in the evening than it does in the dark morning hours. Star patterns change from season to season too. In the Northern Hemisphere, we see Orion high in the winter sky, but in summer we lose part or all of Orion as it dips below the horizon.

These changes should not surprise you. Like the Sun's movement across the sky during the day, star movements in the night sky are the result of our own Earth's movements. Recall that Earth rotates on its axis and orbits the Sun. These movements affect the star patterns you see.

✓ Lesson Checkpoint

1. Name and explain the process inside a star that produces the star's energy.
2. Explain the difference between apparent magnitude and absolute magnitude.
3. **Draw Conclusions** The star Antares is about 520 light-years from Earth, while the star Betelgeuse is about 430 light-years away. Given this information, can you predict which star appears brighter in the night sky? Why or why not?

Guided Inquiry

Investigate How can you make a model to show the motions of planets?

Planets closer to the Sun orbit the Sun more often than planets farther from the Sun. You can make a model to show this pattern.

Materials

cardboard and
drawing compass

colored pencils or markers

white paper

scissors and clear tape

5 round toothpicks

Process Skills

Making and **using a model** of how the planets move can help you form a mental picture of the planets' orbits.

What to Do

1 Draw a circle in the center of the cardboard to represent the Sun. Draw 5 circles around the Sun and make each circle a different color.

Each circle represents an orbit. Actual orbits are not quite circular.

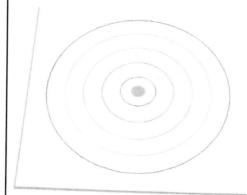

Earth Months Needed for One Orbit

Mercury	3
Venus	7
Earth	12
Mars	23
Jupiter	142

2 Mark 3 evenly spaced dots on the smallest circle. It takes Mercury 3 months to orbit the Sun. In 1 month, it would make $\frac{1}{3}$ of an orbit and would be at the first dot.

Always place the first dot at the "top" position.

3 Use the data in the chart to complete your **model**. Repeat step 2 for Venus, Earth, and Mars. To save time, for Jupiter simply mark 35 dots in the first $\frac{1}{4}$ of its orbit.

Start the flags with each flag on the first dot.

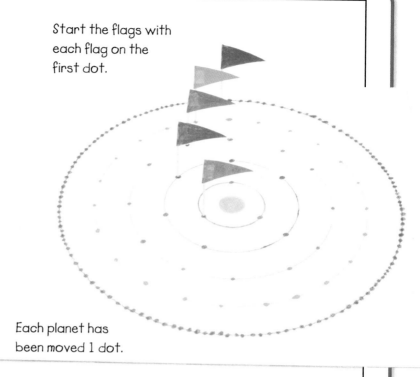

Each planet has been moved 1 dot.

4 Make a planet flag for each orbit. Cut a triangle from white paper. Color it the same color as the planet's orbit. Then tape the triangle to a toothpick.

5 Place each planet flag at the "top" dot of its orbit.

6 Start the planets on their orbits. Move each flag, in turn, counterclockwise by 1 dot. This shows how far each planet would move in 1 month.

7 Move each flag to the second dot in its orbit. Continue to move each flag along dot-by-dot until it has traveled to 12 dots. Record your **observations** in the chart.

Movement of Planets in 12 Months

Planets that made more than 1 orbit	
Planet that made exacly 1 orbit	
Planets that made less than 1 orbit	

Explain Your Results

1. Name two ways the orbits in this **model** are like the orbits of actual planets. Name two ways they are different.
2. Neptune takes 1,964 months to orbit the Sun. How fast do you think it appears to move? Why do you think Neptune was discovered later than the inner planets?

Go Further

Extend your model to include all the planets. Describe the benefits and drawbacks to extending your model.

Scientific Notation and the Planets

You have learned that scientists often use astronomical units to express distances in the solar system. Astronomical units are helpful for comparing distance in space. An AU is the average distance of Earth from the Sun, about 149.6 million kilometers. Written in standard form, the number of kilometers is 149,600,000.

Scientific notation is often used to express very small or very large numbers, like the one above. Scientific notation shows a number as the product of two factors. The first factor is always a number greater than 1 but less than 10. The second factor is always a power of 10.

$$149,600,000 = 1.496 \times 10^8$$

If you multiply 1.496×10^8, the decimal point would move 8 places to the right, so the product would be 149,600,000.

AVERAGE DISTANCE FROM THE SUN								
INNER PLANETS				OUTER PLANETS				
Mercury	Venus	Earth	Mars	Jupiter	Saturn	Uranus	Neptune	Pluto
0.39 AU	0.72 AU	1 AU	1.52 AU	5.2 AU	9.58 AU	19.20 AU	30.05 AU	39.24 AU

What is Venus's average distance from the Sun in kilometers? The table tells us that Venus is 0.72 AU from the Sun.

$$1 \text{ AU} = 1.496 \times 10^8 \text{ km}$$

$$0.72 \times 1.496 \times 10^8 = 1.07712 \times 10^8$$
$$= 107,712,000$$

Multiplying a decimal number by 10^8 will move the decimal point 8 places to the right.

Venus's average distance from the Sun is 107,712,000 km or rounded to the nearest million as 108,000,000 km.

Use the chart on page 572 to answer the questions. For Questions 1–4, give each answer in scientific notation and in standard form.

Find each planet's average distance from the Sun in kilometers.

1. Mercury

2. Jupiter

3. Saturn

4. Which planets are more than 30 times as far from the Sun as Earth is? Find the average distance of each of these planets from the Sun, in kilometers.

5. What is the average distance of Mars from the Sun, in astronomical units? Use this data to write a statement comparing the distance of Mars from the Sun with the distance of Earth from the Sun.

Lab zone Take-Home Activity

Use library resources to find data about five stars. Find the distance of each star from Earth in light years. Put the data for five stars in a chart. Then write each distance in kilometers using scientific notation.

573

Chapter 20 Review and Test Prep

Use Vocabulary

astronomical unit (p.560)	**magnitude** (p. 565)
constellation (p. 568)	**nuclear fusion** (p. 564)
galaxy (p. 559)	**solar system** (p. 560)
light-year (p. 564)	**star** (p. 564)

Use the vocabulary term from above that best completes each sentence.

1. The process that powers stars is ____.

2. Apparent ____ is how bright a star seems to us.

3. The ____ is a useful unit of distance in deep space.

4. Orion is a ____ in the night sky.

5. Distance in the solar system often is measured in a unit called the _____.

6. The____ includes the Sun, planets, and moons.

7. Our Sun is in the ____ known as the Milky Way.

8. A ____ is a huge ball of glowing gases.

Explain Concepts

9. How is star color related to star temperature and its life cycle?

10. Describe the Milky Way Galaxy and Earth's place in it.

11. Explain the process that causes an aging star to swell up into a red giant.

Process Skills

12. **Classify** Suppose you make a chart of the stars in a large constellation. You want to group stars within subsections of the chart. How might you group them in a scientifically meaningful way?

13. **Predict** Suppose a supergiant star collapses. What probably will happen next? Give reasons for your prediction.

14. **Model** Make a scale model of the solar system, using a large sheet of butcher paper or poster paper. Use the distance units from the chart on page 562 to set up your scale. Careful! To position the outer planets on your paper, you will need to space the inner planets closely. Show your scale in a key.

 Draw Conclusions

15. Make a graphic organizer like the one shown below. Use factors from the chapter to draw a conclusion about which star—A or B—is closer to Earth. Star A and Star B have the same apparent magnitude in the night sky. The absolute magnitude of Star B is greater than Star A.

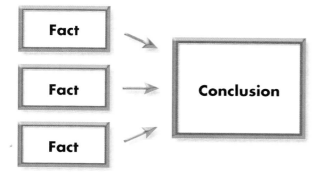

 Test Prep

Choose the letter that best completes the statement or answers the question.

16. An astronomical unit (AU) is defined as
Ⓐ the distance between the Sun and Mercury.
Ⓑ the distance between the Earth and its moon.
Ⓒ the distance light travels in one minute.
Ⓓ the distance between the Sun and the Earth.

17. Our Sun is classified as a
Ⓕ nova.
Ⓖ mid-sized star.
Ⓗ white dwarf.
Ⓘ red giant.

18. Which statement about constellations is true?
Ⓐ Stars move so fast that constellations march across the night sky.
Ⓑ Every constellation represents a particular galaxy.
Ⓒ People in the Northern and the Southern Hemispheres see the very same constellations.
Ⓓ The apparent movement of constellations is the result of Earth's movements.

19. Explain why the answer you chose for Question 18 is best. For each of the answers you did not choose, give a reason why it is not the best choice.

20. **Writing in Science** **Expository**
An analogy compares unlike things to explain a relationship. Think of an analogy to explain the difference between apparent and absolute magnitude of stars. For example, you could use the analogy of viewing skyscrapers in a city skyline. Buildings close to you would look bigger than they really are, while very tall buildings at some distance would look smaller. Write your explanation in a paragraph or two.

PTOLEMY

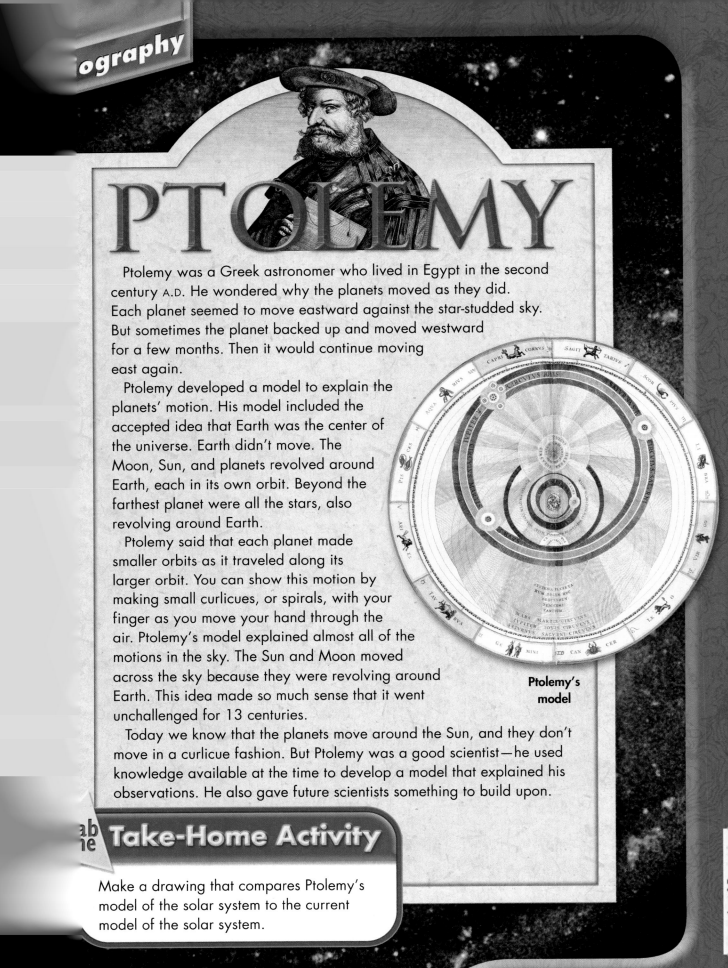

Ptolemy was a Greek astronomer who lived in Egypt in the second century A.D. He wondered why the planets moved as they did. Each planet seemed to move eastward against the star-studded sky. But sometimes the planet backed up and moved westward for a few months. Then it would continue moving east again.

Ptolemy developed a model to explain the planets' motion. His model included the accepted idea that Earth was the center of the universe. Earth didn't move. The Moon, Sun, and planets revolved around Earth, each in its own orbit. Beyond the farthest planet were all the stars, also revolving around Earth.

Ptolemy said that each planet made smaller orbits as it traveled along its larger orbit. You can show this motion by making small curlicues, or spirals, with your finger as you move your hand through the air. Ptolemy's model explained almost all of the motions in the sky. The Sun and Moon moved across the sky because they were revolving around Earth. This idea made so much sense that it went unchallenged for 13 centuries.

Ptolemy's
model

Today we know that the planets move around the Sun, and they don't move in a curlicue fashion. But Ptolemy was a good scientist—he used knowledge available at the time to develop a model that explained his observations. He also gave future scientists something to build upon.

Take-Home Activity

Make a drawing that compares Ptolemy's model of the solar system to the current model of the solar system.

Chapter 21
Technology

online
Student Edition
sfsuccessnet.com

You Will Discover

- what robots are.
- how robots help humans every day.
- what nanotechnology is.
- the advantages and disadvantages of nanotechnology.

How can robots help us now and in the future?

robot

robotics

autonomous robot

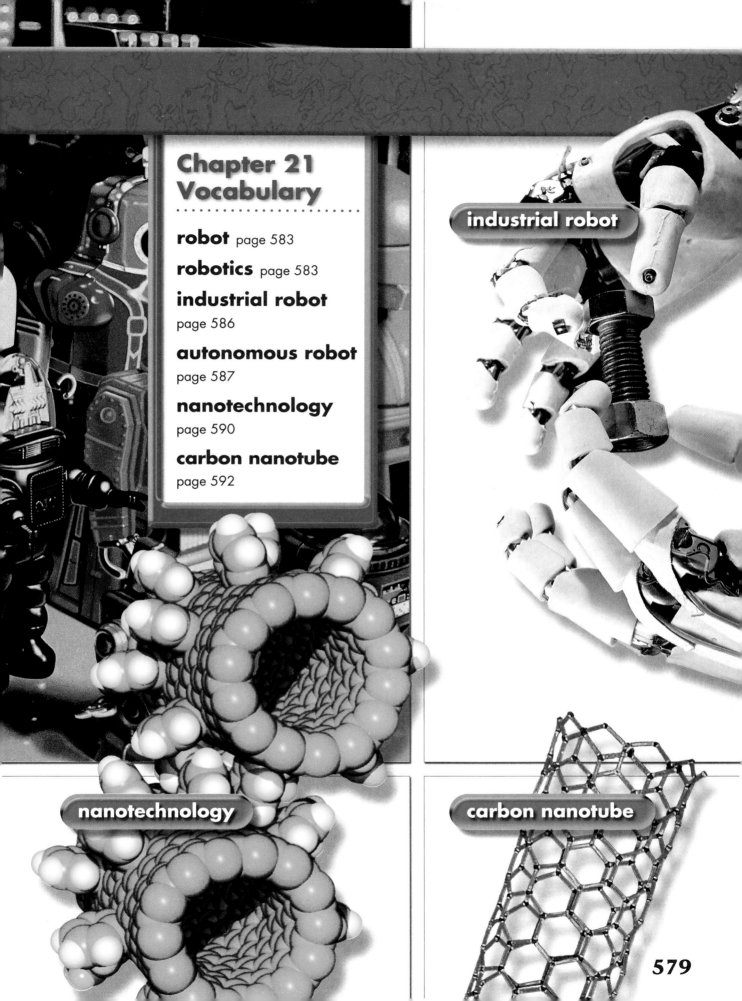

Chapter 21 Vocabulary

industrial robot

nanotechnology

carbon nanotube

579

Explore How can a robot tie a shoe?

Few robots are designed to do simple human tasks. Tying a shoe might be a difficult task for a robot. You can learn why as you try this activity.

Materials

shoe with laces

timer

2 plastic bags

2 clothespins

4 craft sticks

masking tape

What to Do

1. Record how long it takes you to tie a shoe.

2. Repeat but limit the feedback and information you get from your senses. Allow only 5 minutes for each try.
   - Tie a shoe with your eyes closed.
   - Tie a shoe with plastic bags on your hands.

3. Use a clothespin as a **model** of a robot's hand. Tie a shoe using clothespins for hands. Record your time.

4. Act as a model of a robot with few moving joints. Tape craft sticks to your thumbs and forefingers. Tie a shoe. Record your time.

Process Skills

Using a model can help you understand why some activities might be difficult for a robot.

Explain Your Results

1. What could you do that your **model** of a robot could not do?

2. Write a main idea statement that tells what you learned in this activity. Give details to support your statement.

How to Read Science

Reading Skills

TARGET SKILL Main Idea and Details

Sometimes the **main idea** of a reading passage is not directly stated. In those cases, the author gives **details** or key ideas that lead you to the main idea. You must put these ideas together and infer the main idea.

- Identify important details and key ideas.

- Put the ideas together into a general statement about the ideas.

Science Article

Robot Revolution

Robots may someday be the only workers in a factory. Robots can work 24 hours a day without tiring. They can do tedious jobs that would bore the humans they replace. In places that might be dangerous for humans, robots can work without being harmed. Robots can go places that humans can't, including distant planets.

Apply It!

Make a graphic organizer like this one. List the **details** from the article. Then write a sentence that **communicates** the **main idea.**

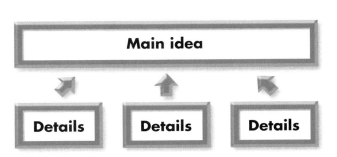

Main idea

Details	Details	Details

You stare in amazement. You had no idea that there could be so many different robots! Some are so tiny that they can fit in the palm of your hand. Others are tall—almost as tall as you are. Yet all look like humans in some way. Each has its own style of legs, arms, and head. Do all robots look like this?

AudioText

What is a robot?

A robot is a machine that is able to get information from its surroundings and do physical work. Today robots are used in industry and medicine, for exploration, and at home. Robots have become more complex over time.

Robots and Robotics

You may immediately recognize the figures on these pages as robots, but what about the thousands of other robots that work for us? Many look far different than these robots. Often they do jobs too dangerous, repetitive, boring, or delicate for humans to do. There are robots working 24 hours, 7 days a week to assemble automobile body panels and then weld them together. Other robots have a real sweet job—they draw chocolate stripes on cookies. In some hospitals, robot hands help human doctors complete surgeries too precise and sensitive for human hands alone. And what about robots working for homemakers? Homemakers can use a robot to clean floors or mow lawns.

The wide variety of robots makes forming an exact definition difficult. However, most scientists agree that a **robot** is a machine that is able to get information from its surroundings and do physical work, such as moving or manipulating objects. Often when people talk about robots, they also mention **robotics,** the technology dealing with the design, construction, and operation of robots.

1. ✓ **Checkpoint** What two requirements must a machine meet to be a robot?
2. 🔄 **Main Idea and Details** Give three details to support this statement: Robots can help humans perform tasks more efficiently.

Robot Development

Say the word *robot,* and most people think of the robots they have seen on television or in movies. For decades, these imaginary machines shaped our ideas about what robots should look like and what they should be able to do. Long before we had the technology needed to build robots, the fictional robots inspired us. They produced interest in designing and building real robots, pushing us to see how far our imagination and creativity could take us.

Although the term *robot* is less than 100 years old, people have dreamed about robots and how they might be used for thousands of years. In ancient Greece, Aristotle thought that one day machines might do work for humans by obeying directions. Two thousand years later, we find robots working in nearly every aspect of our lives.

In addition to our imagination, robot development has depended in large part on the development of other technologies, such as computers. As computer systems became more capable, computers smaller, sensors more sensitive, and computer programs more precise, robots have become able to do more complex tasks.

Robot designers work to increase a robot's ability to solve problems. The goal is to design a robot that can survey its environment, analyze data, make a judgment, and then take appropriate action. In turn, improved robot design opens new technologies. For example, a robot capable of moving a mere 0.0000001 centimeter at a time will allow us to manufacture a single molecule, one atom at a time.

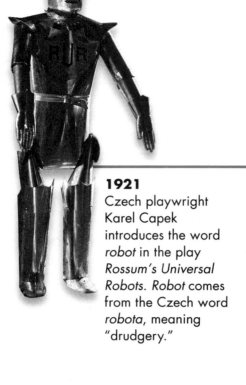

1921
Czech playwright Karel Capek introduces the word *robot* in the play *Rossum's Universal Robots. Robot* comes from the Czech word *robota,* meaning "drudgery."

2000
The latest robots that resemble humans appear. They can perform tasks much like humans, including climbing stairs.

1. ✔**Checkpoint** Compare and contrast Capek's 1921 robot shown on the timeline with the 2000 robots.

2. **Art** in Science Draw a robot you would like to have in your home. Show what task you would want it to do. Then trade drawings with a partner. Evaluate your partner's robot design.

~270 B.C.
Greek engineer Ctesibus builds organs and water clocks with movable figures.

1739
Jacques Vaucanson, a French engineer, creates an automatic duck that can drink, eat, and perform other functions.

1801
Joseph-Marie Jacquard, a French weaver, invents a method of controlling looms using cards with holes punched in them.

1951
The first remote-operated, jointed arm handles radioactive materials for the Atomic Energy Commission.

1939–1940
A mechanical man and dog appear at the New York World's Fair.

1961
The first industrial robot begins work in an automobile factory.

1970
Shakey, the first mobile robot with vision, figures out how to move around obstacles.

1985
The first robot-aided surgery is performed.

1994
Dante II, a six-legged walking robot, explores Mt. Spurr volcano in Alaska and collects samples of volcanic gases.

2001
The *Space Station Remote Manipulator System (SSRMS)* begins to complete assembly of the International Space Station.

2002
Researchers develop a robotic assistant for the elderly.

1997
NASA's *Pathfinder* lands on Mars and sends the *Sojourner* rover to explore the Martian landscape.

2004
NASA Mars rovers *Spirit* and *Opportunity* land on the red planet.

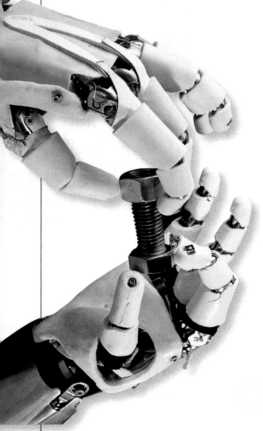

The elbow of this welding robot allows the welding torch to be handled in almost the same ways in which a human would handle it.

Robots in Industry

Nearly 90 percent of today's robots work in factories, more than half of them in automobile factories. Robot arms weld, paint, iron, assemble, pack, inspect, and test manufactured parts. An automatically controlled **industrial robot** can handle several products or items at a time and can be programmed to complete several different tasks.

The most common kind of industrial robot is the robotic arm, which is controlled by a computer. Many industrial robots have "joints" that are very similar to a human arm. You can see in the picture below that a robotic arm has a shoulder, elbow and forearm. A human arm can pivot in seven different ways. This kind of robotic arm can pivot in six different ways.

Different parts attached to the robotic arm enable it to perform specific tasks. For example, the robotic hands shown to the right can be attached to a robotic arm to turn a screwdriver or a bolt. Other attachments might be drills, spray painters, or welding tools.

A robot assigned to weld has three arm movements and three wrist movements. It also has position sensors, making it possible to "teach" the robot how to weld. A human operator leads the robot through the motions necessary to weld a specific location. Sensors on the robot's joints record the twists, turns, and other motions. The robot's computer saves the information, allowing the robot arm to repeat the motions exactly.

Similar directions guide robots to place silicon chips onto circuit boards and then solder them. In fact, the same type of information can direct a robot to pick up a delicate muffin from one moving conveyor belt, turn the muffin in the right direction, and finally place it in a box on a second moving conveyor belt.

This robotic hand is made of metal pieces that are moved by tiny motors.

A Mechanical Arm

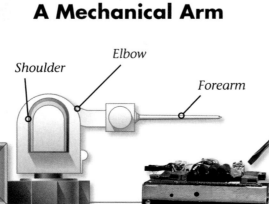
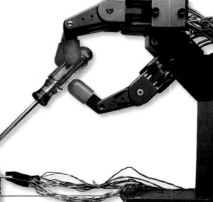

Base

Shoulder

Elbow

Forearm

While industry leads the way in robot use, many robots work in exploration. Robots that are used to explore can be placed into one of two categories. One category includes the remotely operated vehicle (ROV or rover). NASA's Mars missions have used rovers *Sojourner*, *Spirit*, and *Opportunity*. A human operator decided in which direction and how fast each rover should move. The operator then sent signals to the rover describing each move to make.

Rovers search sewers, pipes, collapsed mineshafts, and heating and cooling ducts—places humans cannot go. Rovers investigate and defuse bombs and examine areas contaminated by radioactive materials—jobs far too dangerous for humans.

The second category of exploring robot is an **autonomous robot.** This type of robot acts without direct supervision. It can "decide" whether to travel over a rock or around it. One autonomous robot being developed at NASA is the Personal Satellite Assistant, or PSA. The robot is about the size of a softball. It has sensors for monitoring conditions in a spacecraft, such as the amounts of oxygen, carbon dioxide, and other gases. It can monitor the amount of bacterial growth in the spacecraft too. Sensors also keep tabs on air temperature and air pressure. The camera can be used to video conference. Navigation sensors and other parts enable the robot to move by itself throughout the spacecraft. According to NASA, the robots will function as another set of "eyes, ears, and nose" for the crew.

NASA's Personal Satellite Assistant, or PSA

1. ✓**Checkpoint** Describe two kinds of robots used for exploration.

2. **Writing** in Science **Expository**
New technologies sometimes result in job loss when robots do jobs people used to do. Do you think technologies that cause job losses should be used?

Robots in Medicine

Sending robots to explore space and other locations led to another robot function—using them to routinely travel between locations. Hospitals employ these messenger robots to carry supplies, equipment, and medications from one location to another.

Messenger robots are not the only robots in a hospital. Robotic surgeons—robotic hands moved by a human surgeon's hands—are now being used in hospitals around the world. Doctors can control the robots by mechanical devices or voice activation. In many operations, human hands cannot be as precise as robotic hands. Robot-assisted surgery results in smaller scars, less pain, and shorter hospital stays.

In one robotic system, the doctor sits at a control center, which is a few feet from the patient. A camera placed inside the patient sends 3-D images of the operation area and the surgical instruments to the doctor at the control center. The doctor controls the surgical instruments by moving the controls in much the same way a person moves a joystick.

In another use, robots act as patients for medical students. The robots are programmed to show a set of symptoms and then respond to treatment, including surgery and medication. Some robots are programmed to "die" if they receive improper or inadequate treatment.

Robots are tackling another problem—helping doctors check on their patients when they can't actually visit them. The robot contains a video screen on which the doctor's face appears. A video camera acts as the robot's eyes and ears. Doctors can interact with their patients via the robot using a live computer-video hookup. The goal is not to replace human doctors but instead to enable doctors to interact with their patients no matter where the doctor is.

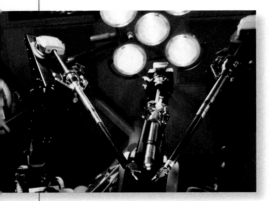

The hands of the surgical robot are capable of more precise movements than a human surgeon's hands.

Human hands guide the hands of a robotic surgical system during precision surgery.

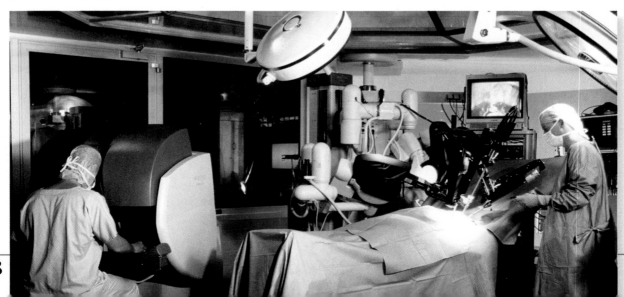

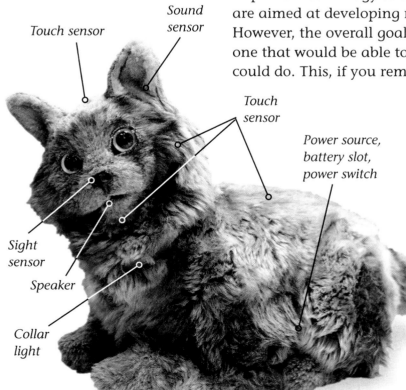

Game robots, like rovers, are remote controlled. However, information gained while working and playing with these robots can help develop completely robotic players for other games or sports.

Robots at Home

You don't have to visit a factory, Mars, or a hospital to see robots in action. In your own home, you can watch popular television programs in which home-built robots challenge one another in an arena. Toy makers offer robot kits that encourage the construction of dozens of interesting robot creations. You may be familiar with the cute, furry robots and the robotic dogs that are made just for entertainment. Given the success of these robots, researchers are working on making a doll-like robot able to perform dozens of movements on its own.

Some companies want to develop a robot that will act as a household companion. This robot would be able to move about the home easily. It would be available to help with tasks, such as giving medication and taking out the garbage. Perhaps such a robot could be programmed to provide care for an elderly or less able person. It could monitor the person's time spent in the kitchen or bathroom, watching television or napping. If any actions seemed out of the ordinary, the robot would dial an emergency number and alert an attendant.

It's clear that robots are here to stay. Each new robot generation will perform new and more complex tasks with less hands-on direction. Large universities, research corporations, and government agencies will rely on improved technology to build these robots. Today's efforts are aimed at developing robots to perform specific tasks. However, the overall goal is to make a universal robot— one that would be able to do almost everything a human could do. This, if you remember, was Aristotle's prediction.

A Robotic Pet

Touch sensor

Sound sensor

Touch sensor

Power source, battery slot, power switch

Sight sensor

Speaker

Collar light

✓ Lesson Checkpoint

1. What kinds of jobs do robots do that humans cannot do?

2. 🎯 **Main Idea and Details** Explain how an autonomous robot solves problems.

3. **Writing in Science**
   Expository What are some human needs that you think robots could not provide solutions for? Explain your answers in a paragraph.

589

What is nanotechnology?

Nanotechnology deals with materials and machines that are measured in nanometers.

Very, Very Small Technology

People dreamed of robots and what they might do long before they were actually developed. Sometimes scientists accidentally stumble into technologies that offer possibilities beyond our wildest dreams. One of the newest technologies, nanotechnology, seems to offer just such possibilities. **Nanotechnology** is the very small-scale technology that deals with materials and processes on a scale best measured in nanometers. A nanometer is a measure of length that is one billionth the length of a meter.

Researchers claim that nanotechnology will allow us to build the materials we want, atom by atom. They hope to do this by lining atoms up in a specific arrangement until they form the desired shape. Does handling atoms one at a time sound too fantastic? As you can see in the picture below, scientists have already done it!

In addition to getting each atom in the correct location, this new technology should allow scientists to make almost any material—as long as its construction follows the laws of physics. The manufacturing costs should not be much more than the cost of the raw materials and the energy used during the manufacturing process.

Two challenges must be met before nanotechnology succeeds. First, scientists have to find a way to move an atom so that it is placed precisely. Scientists know that robots can be precise, so they might look to a nano-sized robotic arm to pick and position each atom.

The second challenge scientists face is finding a way to pick and position billions and billions of atoms. If they are building something atom-by-atom, they will need a lot of robotic arms to put together nano-sized parts into larger parts. More robots will put together the larger parts into still larger parts, eventually forming a product we can actually see.

Scientists hope to build nanogears such as this.

In 1990, researchers moved 35 xenon atoms, one at a time, arranging them to form letters.

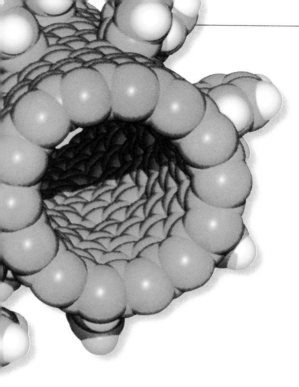

Nanotechnology Applications

Scientists have not yet been able to build many things atom-by-atom. But they have had success changing some existing materials. Researchers have found that they can change certain molecules, called nanopores, to meet their needs. For example, nanopore material can act like a sponge, absorbing mercury or lead from polluted water supplies.

Nanoshells may be the future's best way to fight cancer. Nanoshells are about 120 nanometers in size—that's 1,500 times smaller than a human hair. The shells are injected into a tumor. Then the tumor area is heated. Temperatures inside the tumor become high enough to damage the cancer cells. But they don't damage normal cells in the same area. Nanoshells may be used to deliver cancer drugs to specific parts of the body. Many cancer drugs are harmful not to just cancer cells, but to normal body cells as well. Using nanoshells would limit the body's exposure to harmful substances in the drugs.

Another medical application involves nanocrystals that give off specific colors of light. Researchers can tag chromosomes with these crystals. When the patient's blood sample is exposed to a specific type of light, the nanocrystals glow in response. Researchers can use results from the process to get information about a person's susceptibility to lung cancer.

Scientists are developing procedures to use nanopores to sequence DNA.

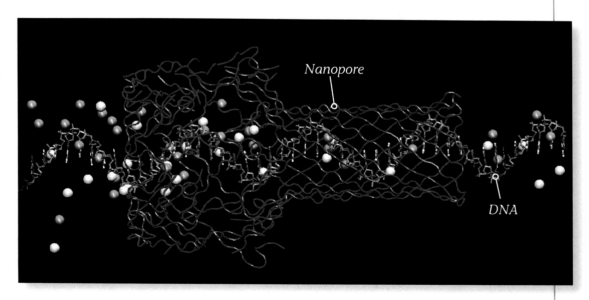

Nanopore

DNA

1. ✅ **Checkpoint** What is nanotechnology?
2. Describe two applications of nanotechnology.

Carbon Nanotubes

For hundreds of years people have known that the element carbon exists in three different forms—diamond, graphite, and "amorphous" carbon. In 1985, scientists discovered a fourth form of carbon with individual molecules that are made up of 60 carbon atoms. These molecules are called buckyballs. Study the pictures below to compare the arrangement of atoms in these forms of carbon.

Then in 1991, researchers found a fifth type of carbon molecule. In this molecule, carbon atoms in six-sided rings arrange themselves in the shape of a tube. The size of the molecule is about a nanometer. This form of carbon is called a **carbon nanotube.**

The properties of diamonds are very different from those of graphite. Recent studies show that carbon nanotubes have properties that are different from both graphite or diamond. For example, carbon nanotubes are exceptionally stiff and can be one hundred times tougher than steel at one-sixth the weight.

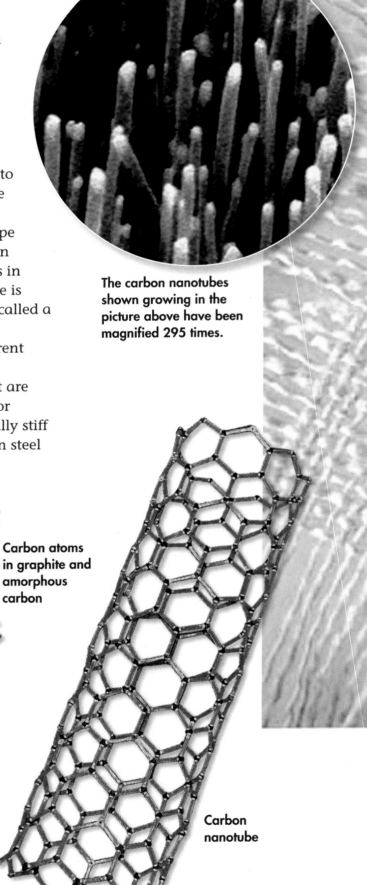

The carbon nanotubes shown growing in the picture above have been magnified 295 times.

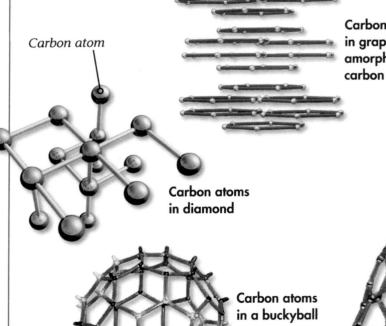

Carbon atom

Carbon atoms in graphite and amorphous carbon

Carbon atoms in diamond

Carbon atoms in a buckyball

Carbon nanotube

Fibers of carbon nanotubes (black in swatch above) can be woven into fabrics that can store energy, receive radio signals, or act as sensors. These fabrics can track the body movements of athletes, dancers, and soldiers who wear them.

The carbon nanotube's electrical properties are astounding. Merely twisting a carbon nanotube can change it from an electrical conductor as efficient as copper to a less efficient conductor similar to silicon. In addition, carbon nanotubes conduct heat better than silicon. Silicon is used in making computers and transistors for electronic equipment. These properties of nanotubes lead researchers to think that it may be possible to produce ultra-small transistors and other electrical devices. These devices might be ten times smaller than those in use today.

Benefits and Risks

At this time, nanotechnology promises enormous benefits—from custom-designed materials to ultra-small computers. But what are the risks? As scientists take advantage of custom molecules, they will need to find out whether the molecules will harm the environment. Ultra-small computers will help design better microphones, cameras, and tracking devices. But people will have to decide how to use these inventions for their own security without giving up privacy. Also, society will need to decide how to use nanotechnology to bring better health care, agricultural practices, and manufacturing knowledge to our own country and others.

✔ **Lesson Checkpoint**

1. Name two risks associated with nanotechnology.
2. **Math in Science** What is the size of a nanometer in terms of a centimeter?
3. **Writing in Science** **Persuasive** Write a letter to the editor of your local newspaper explaining whether you think the public ought to have a say in how nanotechnology is used. Explain why.

Investigate How can you make a model of a robot arm?

People who design and build robots to reach, lift, and hold items often use the human arm as a model.

Materials

3 posterboard strips

metric ruler

hole punch

2 fasteners

dowel with hook

3 large paper clips

 clay and string

 rubber band

Process Skills

Making a model of a robot arm can help you form a mental picture of how robots are constructed.

What to Do

1. Use a hole punch to make a hole 2 cm from the ends of each posterboard strip.

2. Use 2 fasteners to join the three strips together.

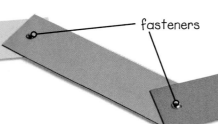
fasteners

3. Put the hook that is on the dowel through the hole in one end of your **model** of a robot arm.

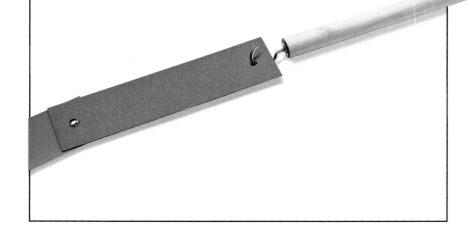

4 Bend a large paper clip into an *S* shape. As shown, put the top part of the *S* into the hole with the hook.

5 Make a clay ball and stick a paper clip into it. Put it on the table along with another paper clip, a rubber band, and a string.

6 Try to pick up each object using the robot arm. Record the number of tries needed to pick up each object.

Move the dowel to make the hook move.

Stop after ten tries. Record the number of tries you make.

This part should not move.

Object	Number of Tries
Clay ball with paper clip	
Paper clip	
Rubber band	
String	

Explain Your Results

1. Which objects were easier to pick up using the robot arm? Why?

2. Name two ways in which this **model** is not like a real robot arm.

Go Further

How could you modify your robot arm so that it could pick up an empty plastic cup? Decide what changes you would make and devise a plan for testing your improved robot arm.

The Mathematics of
NANOTECHNOLOGY

You have been learning about nanotechnology, which involves technological developments on a very small scale. The prefix *nano* means "one billionth." So, a nanometer (nm) equals one billionth of a meter, or one millionth of a millimeter. Look at the size of 1 millimeter on a metric ruler. A nanometer is one millionth of that size!

The chart below gives the exponential form of very small numbers.

Word Form	Standard Form	Exponential Form
1 thousandth	0.001	10^{-3}
1 ten-thousandth	0.0001	10^{-4}
1 hundred-thousandth	0.00001	10^{-5}
1 millionth	0.000001	10^{-6}
1 ten-millionth	0.0000001	10^{-7}
1 hundred-millionth	0.00000001	10^{-8}
1 billionth	0.000000001	10^{-9}

Here's another way to think of the size of a nanometer. A millimeter is one thousandth of a meter (0.001 m); a micrometer is one thousandth of a millimeter (0.001 mm) and a nanometer is one thousandth of a micrometer (0.001 μm).

$$0.001 \times 0.001 \times 0.001 = 0.000000001$$
$$10^{-3} \times 10^{-3} \times 10^{-3} = 10^{-9}$$

In nanotechnology, it is important that tiny robots, called nanorobots, be able to make copies of themselves repeatedly. This is called exponential assembly.

For example, in one process starting with one nanorobot, each nanorobot makes three copies of itself in a day and then stops working. How many nanorobots will be made on Day 4?

The number of nanorobots will increase by powers of 3.

Day	0	1	2	3	4
Power of 3	3^0	3^1	3^2	3^3	3^4
Number	1	3	9	27	81

Use what you've learned to answer each question.

1. You have read that a nanoshell is about 120 nanometers in size. Write this measure in meters, using standard form. Show how you found your answer.

2. A process starts with one nanorobot that makes three copies of itself in a day and then stops working. How many nanorobots will be made on Day 8? Day 10? Copy and extend the chart above to help you find your answer.

3. In the first step of one assembly process, a great number of very small parts are assembled into larger parts. Then these parts are assembled into larger parts, and the step is repeated over and over. If the size of the parts doubles for each step, how many steps would be needed to go from a part that is 1 nanometer in size to a part that is at least 1 millimeter in size? Use a calculator or copy and continue the chart until you find the answer. (Remember: 1 mm = 1,000,000 nm)

Step	0	1	2	3	4
Power of 2	2^0	2^1	2^2	2^3	2^4
Number	1	2	4	8	16

Lab zone **Take-Home Activity**

Use library resources to find more information about nanotechnology. Make a poster or write a story about the possible benefits of nanotechnology in the future. Use your imagination together with the facts you have found.

Use Vocabulary

autonomous robot (p. 587)	**nanotechnology** (p. 590)
carbon nanotube (p. 592)	**robot** (p. 583)
	robotics (p. 583)
industrial robot (p. 586)	

Use the term from the list above that best completes each sentence.

1. The technology dealing with robots is called _____.

2. A machine able to get information from its surroundings and do physical work is a(n) _____.

3. A robot that can act without direct human supervision is a(n) _____.

4. If a robot is automatically controlled, can handle several products at once, and can be programmed to complete several different tasks, it is a(n) _____.

5. The technology that deals with the materials and processes in terms of one-billionth of a meter is _____.

6. The most recently discovered form of carbon with properties far different from those of diamonds and graphite is a(n) _____.

Explaining Concepts

7. Explain why robots are better at some jobs than human workers are.

8. What must a true robot be able to do without human direction?

9. What problems must scientists solve before nanotechnology can provide the benefits it seems to promise?

10. Explain how technology such as computers has influenced the development of robots.

11. Describe the structure of a buckyball.

12. How are Mars rovers *Spirit* and *Opportunity* different from autonomous robots?

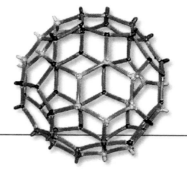

13. Forming Questions and Hypotheses
What question do you have about robots that could be answered by doing an experiment? Write your question as a statement that can be tested by an experiment.

14. Infer Why might a surgeon suggest that the operation you need is best performed with the aid of a robot?

 **Main Idea and Details**

15. Make a graphic organizer like the one shown below. Fill in details about the main idea.

Robots can perform human tasks.

| Detail | Detail | Detail |

Test Prep

Choose the letter that best completes the statement or answers the question.

16. Today most robots work in
Ⓐ hospitals.
Ⓑ space exploration.
Ⓒ industry.
Ⓓ home entertainment.

17. Carbon atoms arranged in six-sided rings to form tubes are
Ⓕ buckyballs.
Ⓖ graphite.
Ⓗ carbon nanotubes.
Ⓘ diamonds.

18. Which is a property of carbon nanotubes that might make it possible for them to replace silicon in electronic equipment?
Ⓐ They're poor conductors of heat.
Ⓑ They glow when hit by a light.
Ⓒ They can change from an efficient electrical conductor to a poor one.
Ⓓ They can assemble themselves.

19. Explain why the answer you chose for Question 17 is best. For each of the answers you did not choose, give a reason why it is not the best choice.

20. Writing in Science **Narrative**
Write a short story in which a robot is a hero because it saved people from one of the dangers of nanotechnology.

David Pieri
VOLCANOLOGIST

How could a love for geology take you to the plains of Mars? And from Mars, how do you arrive on the slopes of a Hawaiian volcano? Ask David Pieri.

Pieri's first job after studying geology in college was with NASA. He joined the Jet Propulsion Laboratory in California in 1979. One of his projects was working with the robots that examined the surface of planet Mars. With other scientists, Pieri studied the images of Mars that the robots took. He used his experience with Earth's geology to try to understand how Mars came to look as it does.

More recently, Pieri has concentrated on volcanoes. He has studied volcanoes from Europe to Hawaii. His experiments concentrate on explosive volcanic eruptions in the northern region of the Pacific Ocean. Pieri flies robot airplanes around the volcanoes to gather information about the volcanoes. Because the clouds of ash from a volcano are very dangerous for an airplane, Pieri's team flies robot aircraft through the ash that volcanoes eject.

Ash from volcanoes also can be dangerous for commercial airplanes. Pieri's project goal is to learn how ash spreads from an exploding volcano so that flying can be made safer for everyone.

Lab zone Take-Home Activity

Design a robot to study an erupting volcano. What would a robot be used to study? Why would scientists need this information?

Unit D Test Talk

Write Your Answer

Short-answer test questions require you to write your answer. Write down your thoughts in complete sentences.

Earth's axis is tilted compared to its orbit around the Sun. As Earth **revolves,** sometimes its Northern Hemisphere leans toward the Sun. Other times, it is leaning away from the Sun. This causes the seasons of the year.

When the North Pole is leaning toward the Sun, it is summer in the Northern Hemisphere. Summer is warmer than other seasons, because sunlight hits the Northern Hemisphere more directly at that time. At the same time, the South Pole is tilted away from the Sun, so sunlight there hits Earth at a greater angle. Temperatures are colder, and the southern Hemisphere is having winter.

At times as Earth moves around the Sun, it is tilted neither toward or away from the Sun. Instead it is tilted in the direction it is traveling. We know these seasons as spring and fall.

Regions of Earth near the **equator** do not have these seasonal differences. The regions receive direct sunlight all year.

When answering test questions, write down what you know. Do not leave an answer blank. Even if you do not know the entire answer, you might earn some points for what you write down.

Use What You Know

1. How does the angle at which sunlight hits Earth differ as Earth travels around the Sun?

2. Why are winter temperatures colder than the temperatures in summer?

3. In the passage, what does the word *revolve* mean?

4. Why don't areas near the equator experience winter and summer? Explain.

Unit D Wrap-Up

Chapter 19

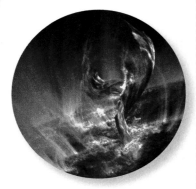

What are the effects of the movement of Earth and the Moon?

- The movement of the Moon around Earth causes the Moon's phases.
- Earth's tilt and orbit around the Sun cause seasons.
- The positions of the Sun, Earth and Moon can cause eclipses.

Chapter 20

What is Earth's place in the universe?

- Earth's Sun is only one of many stars in the universe.
- Earth's solar system is part of the Milky Way Galaxy.
- Earth is the third planet from the Sun.

Chapter 21

How can robots help us now and in the future?

- Robots help people in industry, exploration, and medicine and at home by gathering information and doing work.
- Scientists are working on making robots from individual atoms.

Performance Assessment

Moon Phases

What causes phases of the Moon? Make a model of the Sun, Earth, and its Moon. Use a flashlight, a lump of clay, a straw, and two plastic foam balls—one four times larger than the other. Label the smaller ball *Moon.* Label the larger one *Earth.* The flashlight can be the Sun. Place the straw in the Earth ball, and attach it to a table with the clay. Shine the flashlight on Earth as you move the Moon around Earth in its orbit. What happens to the Moon as it orbits Earth?

Read More About Life Science

Look for books like these in the library.

Experiment How does a sunscreen's SPF relate to its effectiveness?

While the ozone layer surrounding Earth acts as a barrier to ultraviolet (UV) radiation, some still reaches Earth's surface. UV radiation can cause sunburn, tanning, and aging of the skin. It also increases the risk of skin cancer.

Materials

4 small paper plates

sunscreen lotion

aluminum foil

UV sensitive beads

4 black squares

timer

Process Skills

You **control variables** when you change only one thing in an **experiment**.

Ask a question.

How does the sun protection factor (called SPF) of a sunscreen affect the amount of protection from UV radiation?

no sunscreen / no sun

UV beads are beads that react to UV radiation by changing color.

State a hypothesis.

If UV beads are coated with sunscreens with different SPFs, will the beads coated with a sunscreen that has higher SPF show a smaller color change than UV beads coated with a sunscreen that has a lower SPF? Write your **hypothesis**.

Identify and control variables.

The SPF is the variable that you change. The variable you observe is the amount of color change that will occur in 30 seconds.

Test your hypothesis.

1 Write "no sunscreen, no sunlight" on one plate. Write "no sunscreen, full sunlight" on another paper plate. Label the other two plates with the SPF values of the sunscreens you will test, for example, "SPF 15/full sunlight" and "SPF 45/full sunlight."

SPF 45 / full sunlight

SPF 15 / full sunlight

no sunscreen / full sunlight

2 Place a small dab of sunscreen on a square of aluminum foil. Coat 4 beads with the sunscreen. Put the beads on the plate with the matching label.

3 Repeat with the other sunscreen. Use the same amount of sunscreen.

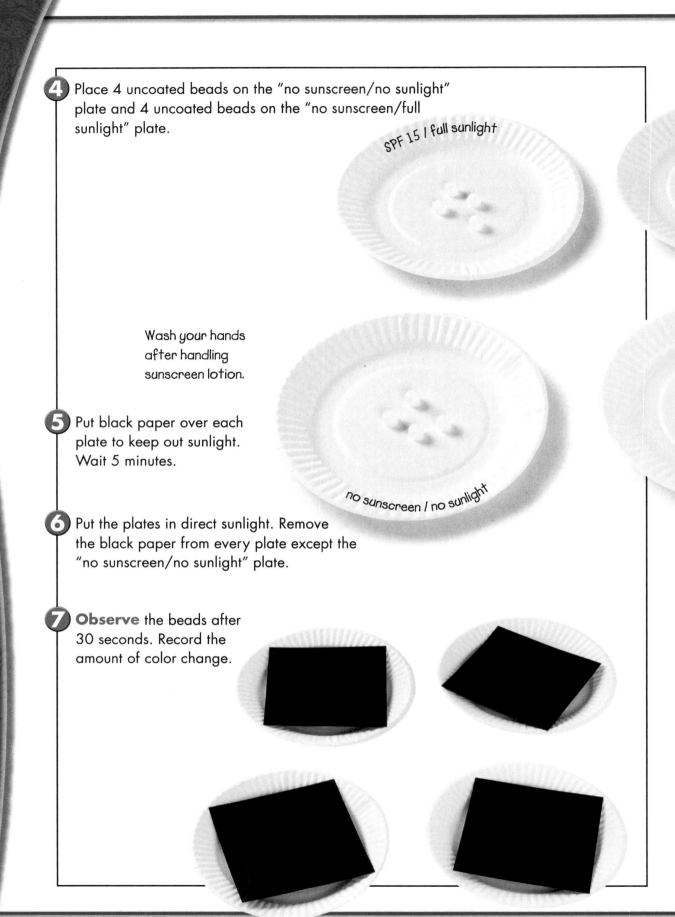

4 Place 4 uncoated beads on the "no sunscreen/no sunlight" plate and 4 uncoated beads on the "no sunscreen/full sunlight" plate.

SPF 15 / full sunlight

Wash your hands after handling sunscreen lotion.

5 Put black paper over each plate to keep out sunlight. Wait 5 minutes.

no sunscreen / no sunlight

6 Put the plates in direct sunlight. Remove the black paper from every plate except the "no sunscreen/no sunlight" plate.

7 **Observe** the beads after 30 seconds. Record the amount of color change.

Collect and record your data.
Use a chart like the one shown to record your data.

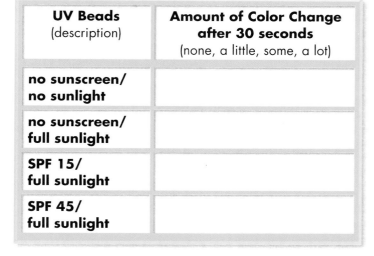

UV Beads (description)	Amount of Color Change after 30 seconds (none, a little, some, a lot)
no sunscreen/ no sunlight	
no sunscreen/ full sunlight	
SPF 15/ full sunlight	
SPF 45/ full sunlight	

Interpret your data.
Think about the SPF of the sunscreens and the amount of color change to the UV beads. Describe the relationship.

State your conclusion.
Draw a conclusion from your data. Does your conclusion agree with your hypothesis? Explain. **Communicate** your conclusions.

Go Further
How might water affect the amount of UV protection provided by a sunscreen? Design and carry out a plan to investigate this or other questions you may have.

Using Scientific Methods

1. Ask a question.
2. State a hypothesis.
3. Identify and control variables.
4. Test your hypothesis.
5. Collect and record your data.
6. Interpret your data.
7. State your conclusions.
8. Go further.

Solar Time

The earliest clocks used the Sun and shadows to tell the time of day.

Idea: Build a sundial and demonstrate how it works.

Robotic Arms

A robotic arm can have few parts, or it can have many.

Idea: Design an experiment to see whether more parts make a robotic arm better.

Crater Creations

When you look at Earth and the Moon, you can see evidence of craters.

Idea: Using sand and rocks, demonstrate how meteors form craters.

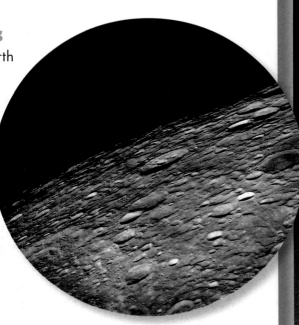

Science Fair **Central** More science fair help
sfsuccessnet.com

EC NTL 10 9 8 7 6 5 4 3

Metric and Customary Measurement

The metric system is the measurement system most commonly used in science. Metric units are sometimes called SI units. SI stands for International System because these units are used around the world.

These prefixes are used in the metric system:

kilo- means *thousand*
1 kilometer equals 1,000 meters

milli means *one thousandth*
1,000 millimeters equals 1 meter

centi means *one hundredth*
100 centimeters equals 1 meter

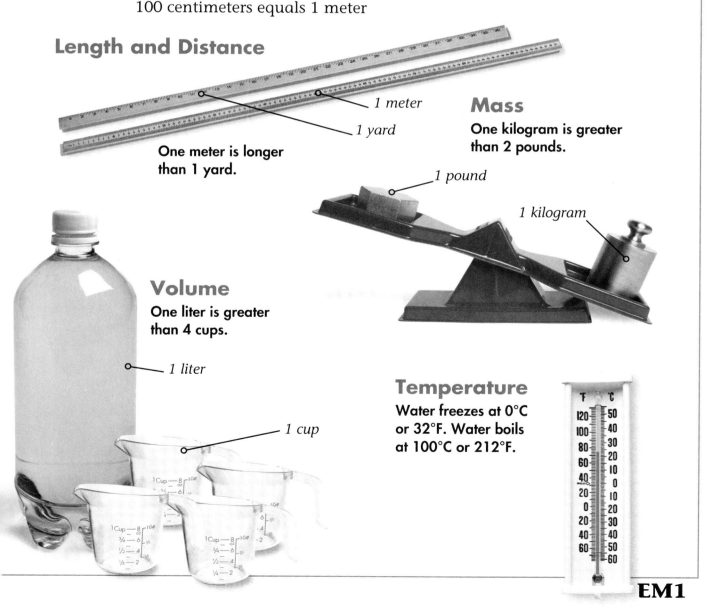

Length and Distance

1 meter
1 yard

One meter is longer than 1 yard.

Mass

One kilogram is greater than 2 pounds.

1 pound

1 kilogram

Volume

One liter is greater than 4 cups.

1 liter

1 cup

Temperature

Water freezes at 0°C or 32°F. Water boils at 100°C or 212°F.

Glossary

The glossary uses letters and signs to show how words are pronounced. The mark ′ is placed after a syllable with a primary or heavy accent. The mark ′ is placed after a syllable with a secondary or lighter accent.

To hear these words pronounced, listen to the AudioText CD.

A

abiotic factor (ā′ bī ′ot ik fak′tər) a nonliving part of an ecosystem (page 146)

acceleration (ak sel′ə rā′shən) the rate at which velocity changes (page 435)

acid precipitation (as′id pri si′ pə tā′shən) rain or snow that is more acidic than normal precipitation (page 307)

adaptation (a′d ap tā′shən) a characteristic that enables an organism to survive and reproduce in its environment (page 8)

air mass (âr mas) a very large body of air that has a similar temperature and humidity throughout (page 336)

air pressure (âr presh′ər) the measure of force with which air particles push on matter (page 328)

alveoli (al vē′ō lī) tiny sacs in the lungs at the end of bronchioles (page 101)

antibody (an′ti bo′d ē) chemicals produced by white blood cells that kill specific pathogens (page 103)

asexual reproduction (ā sek′shü əl rē′prə duk′shen) production of offspring by a single parent (page 56)

astronomical unit (as′trə nä mi kəl yü′nit) the average distance of Earth from the Sun, about 149.6 million kilometers (page 560)

atmosphere (at′mə sfir) the blanket of gases that surrounds a planet (page 327)

autonomous robot (ȯ ton′ə məs rō′bot) a type of robot that acts without direct supervision (page 587)

B

bacteria (bak tir′ē ə) single-celled organisms that do not have a nucleus (page 12)

biome (bī′ōm) a large group of ecosystems with similar climates and organisms (page 148)

biosphere (bī′ə sfir) part of the Earth that can support living things (page 7)

biotic factor (bī o′t ik fak′tər) a living organism in an ecosystem (page 146)

C

carbon nanotube (kär′bən nan′ō tüb) carbon atoms in six-sided rings that are arranged in the shape of a tube (page 592)

cause (kȯz) the reason something happens (page 85)

cellular respiration (sel′yə lər res′pə rā′shən) the process by which cells combine glucose with oxygen for the release of energy (page 124)

chemical change (ke′mi kəl chänj) the changing of a substance into a completely new substance with different properties (page 376)

chemical property (ke′mi kəl pro′p ər tē) a characteristic that determines how a substance reacts with other substances (page 371)

chemical weathering (ke′mi kəl we′ᵺH ər ing) a change in minerals as they react with substances in the environment, such as water or oxygen (page 272)

chromosome (krō′mə sōm) coiled structure in a cell nucleus that carries information controlling the cell's activities (page 39)

classification (klaʹsə fə kāʹshən) a grouping of things according to their similarities (page 11)

climate (klīʹmit) a pattern of weather that occurs in an area over a long period (page 342)

coal (kōl) a solid fossil fuel (page 306)

community (kə myüʹnə tē) a group of populations that interact with one another in a particular area (page 144)

compare (kəm pârʹ) to show how things are alike (page 5)

competition (komʹpə tisʹhən) the struggle among organisms to survive in a habitat with limited resources (page 176)

compound (komʹpound) a substance composed of two or more elements that are chemically combined to form a new substance (page 400)

compound machine (komʹpound mə shēnʹ) a machine made up of one or more simple machines (page 456)

concentration (konʹsən trāʹshən) a measure of the amount of solute dissolved in a solvent (page 405)

conclusion (kən klüʹzhən) a decision reached after thinking about facts and details (page 213)

condensation (konʹden sāʹshən) the change of state from a gas to a liquid (page 375)

conduction (kən dukʹshən) heat transfer between two objects that touch (page 505)

conductor (kən dukʹtər) a material through which electricity or heat is easily transfered (page 508)

constellation (konʹstə lā shən) a part of the sky containing a certain group of stars (page 568)

continental drift (konʹtə nenʹtl drift) the theory stating that continents are continually moving (page 220)

contrast (kən trastʹ) to show how things are different (page 5)

convection (kən vekʹshən) the transfer of thermal energy by the movement of a liquid or a gas (page 506)

core (kôr) the innermost layer of Earth (page 216)

crust (krust) the outermost solid layer of Earth (page 216)

crystal (krisʹtl) a regular, repeating pattern in which particles of minerals are arranged (page 247)

decomposer (dēʹkəm pōʹzər) an organism that breaks down the chemicals from dead organisms and returns materials to the environment (page 171)

density (denʹsə tē) the amount of mass in a certain volume of matter (page 368)

deposition (depʹə ziʹsh ən) the process of dropping sediments onto a new place after being carried away from another place (page 274)

detail (diʹtāl or dēʹtāl) an individual piece of information that support a main idea (page 141)

diffusion (di fyüʹshən) the movement of a substance from an area of higher concentration to an area of lower concentration (page 36)

DNA a material in a cell's nucleus that stores coded information about how an organism will grow and develop (page 39)

ecosystem (ēʹkō sisʹtəm or ekʹō sisʹtəm) an area in which living things and nonliving parts of the environment interact (page 145)

effect (i fektʹ) what happens as the result of a cause (page 85)

effort force (eʹfərt fôrs) a force applied to the end of a lever to lift a load (page 458)

egg cell (eg sel) sex cell of the female parent (page 62)

electric circuit (i lekʹtrik sèrʹkit) a closed path along which current can flow (page 483)

electric current (i lekʹtrik kèrʹrənt) a flow of electric charge in a material (page 483)

electric motor (i lekʹtrik mōʹtər) a device that changes electrical energy to kinetic energy (page 487)

electromagnetic wave (i lekʹtrō mag netiʹk wāv) light and other forms of energy that travel through space (page 511)

element (elʹə mənt) a substance made of only one kind of atom (page 394)

endocrine gland (enʹdō krən or enʹdō krin gland) an organ that releases hormones directly into the blood (page 96)

endoplasmic reticulum (en′dō plaz′mic ri tik′yə ləm) a network of folded membranes that serves as the cell's transportation system (page 34)

energy (e′nər jē) the ability to cause change or to do work (page 479)

energy pyramid (e′nər jē pir′ə mid) a model that shows the amount of energy available at each level of an ecosystem (page 175)

environment (en vī′rən mənt) all the conditions that surround a living thing (page 144)

enzyme (en′zīm) a chemical that helps break down food into nutrients during digestion (page 98)

epidermis (e′pə dėr′mis) the thin outer layer of plant cells through which water and minerals from the soil enter the root (page 119)

erosion (i rō′zhən) the process by which soil and sediments are transferred from one location to another, usually by wind, water, ice, and gravity (page 273)

fault (fôlt) a break in the Earth's crust at the boundaries where plates slide past each other (page 226)

fertilization (fėr′tl ə zā′shən) the joining of male and female cells in sexual reproduction (page 62)

force (fôrs) a push or pull (page 423)

fossil fuels (fos′əl fyü′əlz) energy sources made from the remains of organisms (page 304)

friction (frik′shən) the force that resists the movement of one surface past another (page 426)

front (frunt) the boundary that forms between air masses (page 336)

fulcrum (ful′krəm) a support on which a lever rests while moving or lifting an object (page 458)

fungi (fung′gī or fung′jī) members of a kingdom of mostly many-celled organisms, some of which break down other organisms; includes mushrooms, yeasts, and molds (page 12)

galaxy (gal′ək sē) a huge grouping of stars (page 559)

gene (jēn) sections of DNA that control the substances the cell makes and when it makes them (page 59)

generator (jen′ə rāt′tər) a device that changes mechanical energy into electrical energy (page 488)

geothermal energy (jē′ō thėr′məl en′ər jē) energy of the heat inside the Earth (page 304)

gland (gland) an organ in the endocrine system that produces a chemical (page 96)

gravitational force (grav′ə tā′shən al fôrs) the force of attraction between objects in the universe (page 428)

guard cell (gärd sel) one of a pair of cells that work together to open and close a leaf's stoma (page 121)

heat (hēt) thermal energy that moves from one substance to another (page 504)

heredity (hə red′ə tē) the passing of traits from parents to their offspring (page 55)

hormone (hôr′mōn) a substance released by an endocrine gland that controls some of the body's functions (page 96)

host (hōst) an organism that is harmed in symbiosis (page 180)

humidity (hyü mid′ə tē) the amount of water vapor in the air (page 332)

humus (hyü′məs) the organic part of soil (page 255)

igneous rock (ig′nē əs rok′) rock formed from lava that has cooled and hardened (page 250)

impulse (im′puls) a message that travels across a neuron and from one neuron to another (page 95)

industrial robot (in dəs′trē əl rō′bot) automatically controlled robot that can handle several products or items at a time and be programmed to complete several tasks (page 586)

inertia (in ėr′shə) the tendency of an object to remain at rest or in constant motion unless a force acts on it (page 437)

inference (in′fər əns) a conclusion reached after thinking about a topic (page 29)

instantaneous speed (in′stən tā′nē əs spēd) an object's speed at any moment (page 434)

insulator (in′sə lā′tər) a material through which heat or electricity is not easily transferred (page 508)

kinetic energy (ki net′ik en′ər jē) the energy of a moving object (page 479)

light-year (līt′yir′) the distance light travels in one year: 9 trillion, 460 billion kilometers (page 564)

lithosphere (lith′ə sfir) the Earth's crust and the solid part of the mantle (page 218)

load (lōd) force of an object on a lever (page 458)

lunar eclipse (lü′nər i klips′) the movement of the Moon into Earth's shadow (page 542)

machine (mə shēn′) any device that helps people do work (page 456)

magnetic domain (mag ne′tik dō mān′) a large number of atoms with their magnetic fields pointing in the same direction (page 484)

magnetic field (mag net′ik fēld) the space around a magnet in which the magnet can exert a force (page 484)

magnitude (mag′nə tüd) the brightness of a star (page 565)

main idea (mān i dē′ə) the most important idea of a reading selection (page 141)

mantle (man′tl) a thick layer of Earth just between the crust and the core that contains most of Earth's mass (page 216)

mass (mas) the amount of matter in an object (page 367)

mechanical weathering (mə kan′ə kəl weᴛʜ′ər ing) breaking down of rock by wind, water, and ice (page 272)

meiosis (mī ō′sis) the process of cell division by which sex cells are formed (page 62)

metamorphic rock (me′tə môr′fik rok′) rock formed when heat, pressure, or chemical reactions change one type of rock into another type of rock (page 250)

meteorologist (mē′tē ə rol′ə jist) a scientist who studies weather (page 336)

mineral (min′ rəl or mi′nərəl) a natural, nonliving solid with a definite chemical structure (page 247)

mitochondria (mī′tə kon′drē ə) parts of cells that convert chemical energy of food into a form that the cell can use (page 34)

mitosis (mī tō′sis) the process in which a cell nucleus divides (page 39)

mixture (miks′chər) a combination of substances in which the atoms of the substances are not chemically combined (page 402)

momentum (mō men′təm) a measure of the force needed to stop a moving object (page 441)

nanotechnology (nan′ō tek nol′ə jē) the very small-scale technology that deals with materials and processes on a scale best measured in nanometers (page 590)

natural gas (nach′ər əl or na′ cha rəl gas) a fossil fuel that is a mixture of gases (page 306)

neuron (nür′on) nerve cell that passes messages throughout the body (page 95)

nonrenewable resource (non′ ri nü′ə bəl ri sôrs′ or rē′sôrs) a resource that cannot be replaced as fast as it is used (page 295)

nonvascular plant (non vas′kyə lər plant) a low-growing plant that does not have tubes to carry materials (page 14)

nuclear fusion (nü′klē ər fyü′zhən) the process in which the nuclei of two or more atoms join to form a single, larger nucleus (page 564)

orbit (ôr′bit) the path of an object that revolves around another object (page 540)

organelle (ôr′gə nel′) a structure that performs specific functions within a cell (page 34)

organic matter (ôr ga′nik ma′tər) any substance that is made of living things or the remains of living things (page 255)

osmosis (oz mō′sis) the diffusion of water across the cell membrane (page 37)

parasite (par′ə sīt) an organism that benefits from symbiosis (page 180)

pathogen (path′ə jən) an organism that causes disease (page 102)

periodic table (pir′ē o′dik tā′bəl) a chart in which all the elements are arranged according to the repeating pattern of their properties (page 396)

petroleum (pə trō′lē əm) a liquid fossil fuel (page 306)

phloem (flō′ əm) part of a plant's vascular system that carries sugars throughout the plant (page 119)

photosynthesis (fō′tō sin′thə sis) the process in which plants use energy from light to make glucose and release oxygen (page 122)

physical change (fiz′ə kəl chānj) the change in the appearance of a substance while its properties stay the same (page 376)

physical property (fi′zə kəl pro′pər tē) properties of matter that can be seen or measured without changing the substance into something else (page 370)

plate boundary (plāt boun′dər ē) an area where plates meet (page 226)

plate tectonics (plāt tek ton′iks) the theory that the Earth's lithosphere is broken into about 20 moving plates (page 224)

population (pop′ yə lā′shən) a group of individuals that belong to the same species and live in the same area (page 144)

potential energy (pə ten′shəl en′ər jē) the energy an object has due to its position (page 479)

predict (pri dikt′) to make a statement about what might happen next (page 165)

radiation (rā′dē ā′shən) the transfer of energy in the form of waves (page 506)

reflection (ri flek′shən) the bouncing of light rays off the surface of a material (page 513)

refraction (ri frak′shən) the bending of light as it passes from one material to another (page 512)

relative humidity (rel′ə tiv hyü mid′ ə tē) the amount of water vapor the air actually contains compared with the amount it could hold at a given temperature (page 332)

renewable resource (ri nü′ə bəl ri sôrs′ or rē′sors) a resource that can be replaced through natural processes almost as fast as it can be used (page 295)

revolve (ri volv′) to move on a path around an object (page 536)

ribosome (rī′bə sōm) a structure in the endoplasmic reticulum that begins the process of making proteins (page 34)

robot (rō′bot) a machine that is able to get information from its surroundings and do work (page 583)

robotics (rō bo′tiks) the technology dealing with the design, construction, and operation of robots (page 583)

rock (rok) a solid, natural material made up of one or more minerals (page 250)

rotate (rō′tāt) to spin around an axis (page 536)

sediment (sə′də mənt) solid particles carried from one place and dropped onto another place (page 271)

sedimentary rock (sə′də men′tə rē rok′) rock formed from layers of sediment that have been cemented together (page 250)

selective breeding (si lek′tiv brē′ding) the process of selecting a few organisms with desired traits to serve as parents of offspring (page 72)

sequence (sē′kwəns) the step-by-step ordering of events (pages 53)

sexual reproduction (sek′shü əl rē′prə duk′shən) reproduction by two parents (page 62)

simple machine (sim′pəl mə shēn′) a tool made up of one or two parts (page 456)

solar eclipse (sō′lər i klips′) an alignment of the Sun, Moon, and Earth in which the Moon blocks the Sun from Earth's view (page 542)

solar system (sō′lər sis′təm) the Sun and the cluster of bodies that travel around it (page 560)

solubility (sol′yə bil′ə tē) the maximum amount of solute that can be dissolved in a solvent at a particular temperature, usually expressed in grams of solute per milliliter of solvent (page 405)

solute (sol′yüt or sō′lüt) a substance that has been dissolved (page 404)

solution (sə lü′shən) one substance dissolved in another (page 404)

solvent (sol′vənt) a substance in which a solute is dissolved (page 404)

species (spē′shēz) a group of very similar organisms whose members can mate with one another and produce offspring that are able to produce offspring (page 8)

speed (spēd) a measure of how fast an object is moving (page 434)

sperm cell (spėrm sel) sex cell of the male parent (page 62)

star (stär) a huge, hot, glowing ball of gas in the sky (page 564)

stoma (stō′ma) a small hole in the epidermis of a leaf through which water and gases pass in and out of the plant (page 121)

succession (sək səs′hən) a series of predictable changes that occur in an ecosystem over time (page 187)

symbiosis (sim′bē ō′sis) a close, long-term relationship between organisms that benefits at least one of the organisms (page 180)

thermal energy (thėr′məl e′nər jē) the total kinetic and potential energy of the particles in a substance (page 503)

transpiration (tran′spi rā′shən) the loss of water from a leaf (page 121)

tropism (trō′pi′z əm) plant behavior caused by growth toward or away from something in the environment (page 129)

vascular plant (vas′kyə lər plant) a plant that has tubes for carrying water and nutrients throughout the organism (page 14)

velocity (və los′ə tē) the speed of an object in a particular direction (page 435)

volume (vol′yəm) the amount of space that something takes up (page 367)

weather (we′ᴛᴈər) the condition of the atmosphere at a particular time and place (page 336)

weathering (we′ᴛᴈər ing) the process of breaking down rock into smaller pieces (page 272)

weight (wāt) a measure of the pull of gravity on an object (page 368)

work (wėrk) to use force in order to move an object a certain distance (page 455)

xylem (zī′ləm) a layer of plant cells that moves water and minerals from the roots to other parts of the plant (page 119)

Index

This index lists the pages on which topics appear in this book. Page numbers after a *p* refer to a photograph or drawing. Page numbers after a *c* refer to a chart, graph, or diagram.

E

water as, 298
Reproduction
asexual, 55, *c*56, 56–57, *p*57
sexual, 62–67
Reproductive system, *c*89
Reptile, 16
fossil of, 221, *p*221
number of, *c*9
Resource. *See* Natural resources; Nonrenewable resource; Renewable resource
Respiration
in carbon dioxide–oxygen cycle, 125
Respiratory system, *c*89, *c*100–*c*101, 101, *c*104
Rest
for healthy muscles and bones, 93
Reuse (three Rs of conservation), 301, *c*310
Revolution
time of Moon's, 536
Revolve, 530
Moon and, 536
Ribosome, 26, *c*34
Richter scale, 229, *c*229
Ridge (ocean), 215, 222, *p*222
River, 271
deposition and, 274, *c*274–*c*275
dissolved minerals in, 275
flooding by, 276, *p*276
sediment in, 275, 276, *p*276–*p*277
River deltas, 276
River systems, 276, *p*276–*p*277
Mississippi, 277, *p*277
Robot, 578, 581
definition of, 583
development of, 584, *c*584–*c*585
exploring with, 587, *p*587
at home, 589, *p*589
in industry, *c*585, 586, *p*586
in medicine, 588, *p*588
types of, 582, *p*582, 583, *p*583
Robotic arm, 586, *p*586
Robotics, 578, 583
Robotic surgeon, 588
Rock, 242
chemical weathering and, 272

clues to past in, 252, *c*252
definition of, 250
erosion and, 273
fossils in, 253, *p*253
magnetism of Mid-Ocean Ridge rocks, 223
mechanical weathering and, 272
metamorphic, 250, *p*251
molten, 245
from Moon, *p*537
sedimentary, 250, *p*250, *p*251
soil formation and, 254–255, *c*254–*c*255, 256
in space, 253, *p*253
Rock cycle, *c*250–*c*251
Roller coaster, 432, *p*432–*p*433
Rolling friction, 426, *c*426
Root, 119, *c*119, 128
in soil, 255, *c*255
Root hairs, 119
Rose, *c*15
Rotate, 530
Moon and, 536
Rotation
time of Moon's, 536
Rough surface
friction and, 426
Rover. *See* Remote controlled vehicle (ROV or rover)
Rudder (sailboat), *c*465
Runner
nervous system of, *c*94–*c*95
Ruska, Ernst, *c*32
Rust, *c*377
Rutherford, Ernest, *c*393

Sachs, Julius von, *c*32
Safety
earthquake, 233, *c*233
in severe weather, *c*338
for viewing eclipses, 542
Sahara Desert, 331
Sailboat, *p*425, *c*464–*c*465
Saint Bernard (dog), 73
Saliva, *c*99
as barrier to pathogens, 102
Salt, 275
as ocean resource, 299
Salt water, 298
San Andreas fault, *p*226

Sand
coastal landforms and, 280
color of, 280
Sandbar, 280
Sandstone, *p*250, *c*252
Sandy soil, 256, *c*256–*c*257
Satellites
GPS and, 227
to measure distance between plates, 225
Saturation point, 405
Saturn, *c*561, *c*563
Savannah, 176
Scaffolded Inquiry
Directed Inquiry, Explore, 4, 28, 52, 84, 116, 140, 164, 212, 244, 268, 292, 324, 364, 388, 420, 452, 476, 500, 532, 556, 580
Full Inquiry, Experiment, 204–207, 356–359, 524–527, 604–607
Guided Inquiry, Investigate, 18–19, 42–43, 74–75, 106–107, 130–131, 154–155, 192–193, 234–235, 258–259, 282–283, 314–315, 344–355, 378–379, 408–409, 442–443, 466–467, 490–491, 514–515, 544–555, 570–571, 594–595
Schist, *p*252
Schleiden, Matthias, *c*32, 33
Schrödinger, Erwin, *c*393
Schwann, Theodor, *c*32, 33
Science Fair Projects, 208, 360, 528, 608
Science Process Skills
Classify, 4, 18–19, 23, 46, 135, 318, 383, 412, 471, 574
Collect Data, 192–193, 207, 470
Communicate, 84, 193, 207, 447
Control Variables, 204–207
Experiment, 519
Form a Hypothesis, 22, 197, 204–207, 447
Identify, 196
Infer, 19, 28, 43, 52, 79, 111, 116, 140, 158, 164, 239, 349, 412, 548, 599
Interpret Data, 75, 154–155, 158, 207, 286, 318

Credits

Illustrations

8-16, 120-134 Sharon & Joel Harris; 32-40 Paulette Dennis AOCA, BScBMC, CMI; 34-40 Robert Ulrich; 38 Bob Kayganich; 50, 66, 168-190, 210-222, 230-233 David Preiss; 51-72 Robert Fenn; 57, 70, 129, 242-255, 593 Tony Randazzo; 82-83, 88-103 Jeff Mangiat; 132, 316, 399, 516 Big Sesh Studios; 139, 149 Adam Benton; 144-152 David Schweitzer; 176, 182-185, 216-232 Precision Graphics; 181, 267, 272-280, 424-440 Clint Hansen; 296-341, 461-464, 536-540. 560-569 Peter Bollinger; 368-376, 403, 505-512 Patrick Gnan.

Photographs

Every effort has been made to secure permission and provide appropriate credit for photographic material. The publisher deeply regrets any omission and pledges to correct errors called to its attention in subsequent editions.

Unless otherwise acknowledged, all photographs are the property of Scott Foresman, a division of Pearson Education.

Photo locators denoted as follows: Top (T), Center (C), Bottom (B), Left (L), Right (R), Background (Bkgd).

Cover:

©Planet Earth/Getty Images, ©Gerry Ellis/Minden Pictures, ©Konrad Wothe/Minden Pictures

Front Matter:

v ©DK Images; xi ©DK Images; xii Getty Images; xiiii ©DK Images; xviii ©Michael & Patricia Fogden/Corbis, (Bkgd) ©T. Allofs/Zefa/Masterfile Corporation, (BR) ©Michael & Patricia Fogden/Minden Pictures; xxv (Bkgd) ©Norbert Wu/Minden Pictures, (BR) ©Gloria H. Chomica/Masterfile Corporation, Courtesy of Vision Research, Inc.; xxix (BL) Getty Images, (TL) Courtesy of Vision Research, Inc.; xxx (TR) ©Leonard Lessin/Peter Arnold, Inc.

Unit A:

Chapter 1: 1 ©Wolfgang Kaehler/Corbis; 2 (T) ©1992 John Cancalosi/DRK Photo, (BL) ©Jeffrey Rotman/Photo Researchers, Inc., (BR) ©DK Images, (T) ©Eric Soder/NHPA Limited; 3 (BL) ©Eye of Science/Photo Researchers, Inc., (BL) ©Chinch Gryniewicz/Ecoscene/Corbis, (CR) ©Wolfgang Baumeister/Photo Researchers, Inc., (TR) ©DK Images; 5 (CR) ©Clouds Hill Imaging, Ltd./Corbis, (Bkgd) ©1992 John Cancalosi/DRK Photo; 6 ©1992 John Cancalosi/DRK Photo; 7 (TL) ©Eric Soder/NHPA Limited, (CR) ©George Bernard/OSF/Animals Animals/Earth Scenes, (BL) ©David Fleetham/Getty Images; 8 (TL) ©Gerry Ellis/Minden Pictures, (BL) ©Jeffrey Rotman/Photo Researchers, Inc., (CL) ©Kennan Ward/Corbis; 9 ©J. Eastcott/Y. Eastcott Film/NGS Image Collection; 10 (TR) ©DK Images, (TL, CL) Jerry Young/©DK Images, (CR) ©George Grall/NGS Image Collection, (BL) Natural History Museum /©DK Images; 12 (BL) ©SciMAT/Photo Researchers, Inc., (CL) ©Clouds Hill Imaging, Ltd./Corbis; 13 (TL) ©Wolfgang Baumeister/Photo Researchers, Inc., (CL) ©Andrew Syred/Photo Researchers, Inc., (TC) ©Eye of Science/Photo Researchers, Inc., (C, BC) ©DK Images, (B) ©Martin Harvey/Peter Arnold, Inc.; 14 ©DK Images; 15 (CR) ©DK Images, (C) ©Mary Rhodes/Animals Animals/Earth Scenes, (CL) ©Chinch Gryniewicz/Ecoscene/Corbis; 16 (CR, BL) ©DK Images, (TL) Andreas von Einsiedel/©DK Images; 17 (B, C) ©DK Images, (TR) ©Norbert Wu/Minden Pictures, (BR) ©Fred Bavendam/Minden Pictures, (TL) ©Franklin Viola/Animals Animals/Earth Scenes; 18 (TR) ©Robert Landau/Corbis, (C, BR) ©DK Images, (CR) Jerry Young/©DK Images, (BC) ©Kevin & Betty Collins/Visuals Unlimited; 20 (Bkgd) ©David Samuel Robbins/Corbis, (L) ©Brian A. Wikander/Corbis, (R) ©Dennis Blachut/Corbis, (R) ©David Cayless/Oxford Scientific Films; 21 (CR) ©Gavriel Jecan/Corbis, (BL) ©Terry Whittaker/Frank Lane Picture Agency/Corbis; 24 (T?) California Academy of Sciences, (Bkgd) ©Rubberball Productions/Getty Images; 25 (Bkgd) ©Eye of Science/Photo Researchers, Inc., (BR) ©David Becker/Photo Researchers, Inc.; Chapter 2: 29 (CR) Science Museum, London/DK Images; 30 ©Janet Foster/Masterfile Corporation; 31 (TL) Hilda Canter-Lund/Freshwater Biological Association, (L) ©Dr. David Patterson/Photo Researchers, Inc., (B) ©Eric Grave/Science Photo Library/Photo Researchers, Inc.; 32 (CL) ©Bettmann/Corbis, (BL) Science & Society Picture Library, (BR) Science Museum, London/DK Images, (CR) ©K. R. Porter/Photo Researchers, Inc., (BR) Photo Researchers, Inc.; 33 (BL) ©Oliver Meckes/Photo Researchers, Inc., (BL) ©Bettmann/Corbis, (TL) ©DK Images; 35 ©DK Images; 37 (BL) ©Nigel Cattlin/Photo Researchers, Inc., (TR) ©Michael Abbey/Photo Researchers, Inc., (CR) ©Runk/Schoenberger/Grant Heilman Photography; 39 ©Andrew Syred/Photo Researchers, Inc.; 41 (TR, BR) ©Lester V. Bergman/Corbis; 42 ©Carolina Biological/Visuals Unlimited; 44 (Bkgd) Custom Medical Stock Photo, (CL) ©Reuters/Corbis, (C) ©Robert Pickett/Corbis, (BR) ©Carolina Biological/Visuals Unlimited, (B) ©Lester V. Bergman/Corbis, (BL) ©Sinclair Stammers/Photo Researchers, Inc.; 45 (BL) ©Carolina Biological/Visuals Unlimited, (Bkgd) ©COLOR-PIC/Animals Animals/Earth Scenes, ©Jim Zipp/Photo Researchers, Inc.; 48 (Bkgd) Getty Images, (BL) Photo Researchers, Inc.;

49 ©E. R. Degginger/Photo Researchers, Inc., ©Biophoto Associates/Photo Researchers, Inc.; Chapter 3: 50 ©American Images Inc./Getty Images; 51 (TR) ©CNRI/Photo Researchers, Inc., (CR) ©Frans Lanting/Minden Pictures, (BR) Tracy Morgan/©DK Images; 54 ©Gavriel Jecan/Getty Images; 55 ©Gavriel Jecan/Getty Images, (BR) ©DK Images; 56 (CL) ©Carolina Biological Supply Company/Phototake, (TL) ©CNRI/Photo Researchers, Inc., (BL) Getty Images; 57 (BR) ©DK Images, (TR) ©Andrew J. Martinez/Photo Researchers, Inc.; 58 ©Andrew Syred/Photo Researchers, Inc.; 59 (TR) ©Gerry Ellis/Minden Pictures, (BR) ©DK Images, (BR) ©DK Images; 60 ©Gerry Ellis/Minden Pictures; 61 ©James King-Holmes/Photo Researchers, Inc.; 62 (BL) ©Frans Lanting/Minden Pictures, (TL) ©David M. Phillips/Photo Researchers, Inc.; 64 (TL) ©David M. Phillips/Photo Researchers, Inc., (T) ©SciMAT/Photo Researchers, Inc.; 65 (TR) ©Fred Bavendam/Minden Pictures, (BR) ©Bill Bachman/Photo Researchers, Inc.; 66 ©American Images Inc./Getty Images; 67 ©M. I. Walker/Photo Researchers, Inc.; 70 ©J. C. Carton/Bruce Coleman Inc.; 72 ©DK Images; 73 (TL, CR) Tracy Morgan/©DK Images; 74 ©Scott T. Smith/Corbis; 76 (Bkgd) ©The Image Bank/Getty Images, (TC) ©Dmitriy Margolin/Acclaim Images, (C, BC) ©ThinkStock/SuperStock; 77 ©ThinkStock/SuperStock; 79 ©CNRI/Photo Researchers, Inc.; 80 JSC/NASA; 81 ©Lester Lefkowitz/Corbis; Chapter 4: 82 ©CNRI/Photo Researchers, Inc.; 86 ©Jay Dickman/Corbis; 88 (BL) ©Science Photo Library/Photo Researchers, Inc., (BC) ©VVG/Photo Researchers, Inc.; 89 (TR) ©A. Syred/Photo Researchers, Inc., (C) ©SIU/Visuals Unlimited; 90 (BR) ©SPL/Photo Researchers, Inc., (CL) ©Dee Breger/Photo Researchers, Inc.; 91 ©P. Motta/Photo Researchers, Inc.; 94 (CR) ©Science Pictures Limited/Photo Researchers, Inc., (CL) ©CNRI/Photo Researchers, Inc.; 99 (TR) ©Omikron/Photo Researchers, Inc., (CR) ©SPL/Photo Researchers, Inc., (BR) ©Eye of Science/Photo Researchers, Inc.; 100 (BL) ©Dr. Richard Kessel & Dr. Randy Kardon/Tissues & Organs/Visuals Unlimited, (C) ©Science Photo Library/Photo Researchers, Inc.; 104 ©RNT Productions/Corbis; 105 (T) ©Kenneth Eward/Photo Researchers, Inc., (TR) ©Asa Thoresen/Photo Researchers, Inc., (CR) ©David M. Phillips/Photo Researchers, Inc., (BR) ©Dr. Richard Kessel & Dr. Randy Kardon/Tissues & Organs/Visuals Unlimited; 106 ©Dr. David M. Phillips/Visuals Unlimited; 108 ©Lester Lefkowitz/Corbis; 109 ©The Image Bank/Getty Images; 112 (Bkgd) ©Stem Jems/Photo Researchers, Inc., (BL) ©Lester Lefkowitz/Corbis, (TR) NASA; 113 ©Steve Satushek/Getty Images, (TR) ©Ted Kinsman/Photo Researchers, Inc.; Chapter 5: 114 (T) ©DK Images, (BL) ©Runk/Schoenberger/Grant Heilman Photography; 115 (BL) ©Ed Reschke/Peter Arnold, Inc., (BR) ©Dr. Jeremy Burgess/Photo Researchers, Inc.; 117 (TR) Brand X Pictures, (Bkgd) ©Dan Suzio/Photo Researchers, Inc., (CR) ©A. Riedmiller/Peter Arnold, Inc.; 118 ©Dan Suzio/Photo Researchers, Inc.; 119 ©Runk/Schoenberger/Grant Heilman Photography; 120 ©Runk/Schoenberger/Grant Heilman Photography, (R) ©DK Images; 121 ©Dr. Jeremy Burgess/Photo Researchers, Inc., ©DK Images; 122 ©DK Images, (BR) ©Dr. Jeremy Burgess/Photo Researchers, Inc.; 124 ©P. Motta & T. Naguro/Photo Researchers, Inc.; 125 (T) ©Bill Brooks/Masterfile Corporation, (TR) ©DK Images; 126 (R) ©Michael Mahovlich/Masterfile Corporation, (TL) ©DK Images; 127 (L) ©Francesc Muntada/Corbis, (TR) ©DK Images; 128 Getty Images; 129 (L) ©Ed Reschke/Peter Arnold, Inc., (TC) ©Robert Calentine/Visuals Unlimited, (TR) ©Adam Jones/Visuals Unlimited; 130 ©Bryan F. Peterson/Corbis; 136 (Bkgd) ©Stone/Getty Images, (CL) ©Photographer's Choice/Getty Images, (L) ©John Miller/Bridgeman Art Library; 137 (Bkgd, CR) ©Larry Williams/Corbis; Chapter 6: 138 (BL) ©Jose Fuste Raga/eStock Photo, (BR) ©Steve Kaufman/Corbis, (BC) ©Gray Hardel/Corbis; 139 ©David Paynter/Age Fotostock; 142 ©Ron Thomas/Getty Images; 143 (CR) ©Gerald L. Kooyman/Animals Animals/Earth Scenes, (L) ©DK Images; 144 ©David Paynter/Age Fotostock; 146 (BL) ©Steve Kaufman/Corbis, (R) ©Jose Fuste Raga/eStock Photo; 147 (TR) Jerry Young/©DK Images, (L) ©Roger Leo/Index Stock Imagery; 150 (BL) ©Kirt L. Hart/Getty Images, (TR) ©Cornelia Doerr/Age Fotostock, (BR) ©Brian Sytnyk/Masterfile Corporation; 151 ©Michael Sewell/Peter Arnold, Inc.; 152 (TR) ©Charlie Ott Photography/Photo Researchers, Inc., (BR) ©Tom Bean/DRK Photo, (CL) ©Paul A. Souders/Corbis, (BL) ©Frank Greenaway/DK Images; 153 (TL) ©Don Pitcher/Stock Boston, (BL) ©Doug Sokell/Visuals Unlimited, (TR) ©Joseph Van Os/Getty Images, (CR) ©DK Images; 154 ©Bill Bachmann/PhotoEdit; 156 (T) ©Heikki Nikki/Oxford Scientific Films, (BC) ©Sally A. Morgan; Ecoscene/Corbis, (B) ©O. Alamany & E. Vicens/Corbis; 157 (TL) ©Royalty-Free/Corbis, (TC) ©Joel W. Rogers/Corbis, (TR) ©Jose Fuste Raga/Corbis; 160 (Bkgd) ©The Image Bank/Getty Images, (R) ©Paul A. Souders/Corbis, (CR) Getty Images, (TL) ©Brand X Pictures/Getty Images; 161 (Bkgd) ©Tui De Roy/Minden Pictures, (TR) ©Mitsuhiko Imamori/Minden Pictures; Chapter 7: 162 (T) ©Renee Lynn/Corbis, (BR) ©Mike Severns/Getty Images, (BR) ©Michael Fogden/Animals Animals/Earth Scenes; 163 (BR) ©DK Images, (BL) ©1999/Gary Braasch; 165 (Bkgd) ©Frans Lemmens/Getty Images, (CR) ©Sally Brown/Index Stock Imagery; 166 (BR) ©DK Images, (Bkgd) ©Frans Lemmens/Getty Images; 167 (TL) ©Royalty-Free/Corbis, (CL) ©Charles Melton/Visuals Unlimited; 168 (L) ©James Balog/Getty Images, (T) ©DK Images, (CL) ©Michael Fogden/DRK Photo, (TL) ©Royalty-Free/Corbis; 169 ©Johnny Johnson/Animals Animals/Earth Scenes; 170 ©DK Images; 171 (B) ©Patrick Johns/Corbis, ©DK Images, (TR) ©B. Murton/Southhampton Oceanography Centre/Photo Researchers, Inc.; 172 (L, BL, TC, C, CL, B, TR, CR, R) ©DK Images, (BR) ©H. Taylor/OSF/Animals Animals/Earth Scenes, (T) Frank Greenaway/©DK Images; 173 (CL, CL, BC, TR, CR, BR, R) ©DK Images, (BL) ©Harold Taylor/OSF Limited; 174 (T, B, CL) ©DK Images, (CR) Kim Taylor and Jane Burton/©DK Images, (CR) Frank Greenaway/©DK Images; 175 (R, CR) ©DK Images, (CL) Dave King/©DK Images; 176 ©Renee Lynn/Corbis; 178 (TL, CL) ©DK Images; 179 (C, BR) ©Michael & Patricia Fogden/Minden Pictures, (T) AP/Wide World Photos, (CR) ©Norbert